W
Bi
IS ALL

BIBLE
STUDY
SERIES

Christians
On the Move

THE BOOK OF ACTS

Based on *What the Bible Is All About* by Dr. Henrietta C. Mears

Written by Bayard Taylor, M.Div.
Dr. Gary S. Greig, Editorial Director for Bible and Theology

Gospel Light
The Bible. Pure and Simple.

Published by Gospel Light
Ventura, California, U.S.A.
www.gospellight.com
Printed in the U.S.A.

Rights for publishing this book outside the U.S.A. or in non-English languages are
administered by Gospel Light Worldwide, an international not-for-profit ministry. For additional
information, please visit www.glww.org, email info@glww.org, or write to Gospel Light Worldwide,
1957 Eastman Avenue, Ventura, CA 93003, U.S.A.

To order copies of this book and other Regal products in bulk quantities,
please contact us at 1-800-446-7735.

CONTENTS

How to Use this Study 5

Preface: Reading the Bible as It Was Meant to Be Read 7

SESSION 1: *Transformers*...13
The Mega-story of Human History (Luke 24; Acts 1)

SESSION 2: *A Shadowy Star* 25
The Holy Spirit in the Bible

SESSION 3: *Happy Birthday, Church*...35
Baptism by Fire (Acts 2)

SESSION 4: *Those Awesome Jesus Women*..45
Partners in the Gospel (Luke–Acts)

SESSION 5: *Marks of the Movement* 57
A Supernatural Fellowship (Acts 3–5:11)

SESSION 6: *Living Out Loud*...69
Dead to Self, Alive to God (Acts 5:12–7)

SESSION 7: *Near Foreigners* 83
Philip, the Forerunner (Acts 8)

SESSION 8: *Was Blind but Now I See*...95
An Amazing U-Turn (Acts 9:1-31)

SESSION 9: *The Strange Sheet* 107
What God Says Is Clean Is Clean (Acts 9:32–12)

SESSION 10: *That Generous Decision* 121
Free from the Law of Moses (Acts 13–15)

SESSION 11: *Come Sail Away* 133
Paul's Missionary Work Among the Gentiles (Acts 16–21:16)

SESSION 12: *An Odd Ending*...147
The Holy Spirit in You! (Acts 21:17–28)

The Mediterranean Region at the Time of Paul (c. AD 70)..............................160

A Timeline of Acts 163

Leader's Tips...171

Bible Reading Plans 173

HOW TO USE
THIS STUDY

In *Christians on the Move*, based on Dr. Henrietta Mears's *What the Bible Is All About*, you will study the book of Acts and discover how Jesus' disciples and apostles continued on Christ's work after He left the earth. During the 12 sessions in this book, you will get a better understanding of how the Holy Spirit empowered the apostles, how the first Church began, how Paul became one of the leading proponents of Christianity, and how these events fit into the bigger picture of God's plan for the ages as laid out from Genesis to Revelation.

Each session begins with an overview of the material that includes the following:

- **Session Focus:** Explains the main theme of the portion of the Bible being examined.

- **Key Verses to Memorize:** Important passages of Scripture that you may want to commit to heart. As Joshua 1:8 states, "Keep this Book of the Law always on your lips; meditate on it day and night, so that you may be careful to do everything written in it. Then you will be prosperous and successful."

- **Weekly Reading:** A listing of the chapters in the Bible that will be covered during the session and a suggested breakdown for how to read the material during a five-day period.

- **Session at a Glance:** Provides an outline for leaders on how to structure the material in a group setting (both 60-minute and 90-minute options are provided).

Before beginning each session, it is recommended that you read the portions of Scripture listed in the weekly reading section of the overview. At the end of each session, you will find a number of personal application and study questions based on these chapters in the Bible and on the background material presented in that session's reading. These questions have been written to allow you to reflect on the material and apply the ideas presented in the session to your life. You can answer these questions individually or incorporate them as part of a small-group discussion.

READING THE BIBLE AS IT WAS MEANT TO BE READ

Dr. Henrietta C. Mears

Dr. Henrietta C. Mears was the director of Christian Education at Hollywood Presbyterian Church for many years and the founder of Gospel Light Publications, Gospel Light Worldwide, and the Forest Home Christian Conference Center in the San Bernardino Mountains of California. In this capacity, Mears put together a highly successful three-year high school curriculum on the whole Bible, which serves as the foundation for this study guide series.

Mears was a modern-day champion of the "Christo-centric" interpretation of the Bible, whereby Christ is considered to be the center of all the themes of both the Old and New Testaments. At a time when others were centered on historicism, the evolution of the idea of monotheism, genre studies or the study of the communities out of which certain writings were presumed to arise, Henrietta steadfastly kept the focus on Jesus. In this persistent attention to the centrality of Jesus Christ, Henrietta was in good company: This same impulse has been found in the best thinkers of the Church throughout the centuries—including Augustine, Basil the Great and John Chrysostom—and it had its start in the Bible itself.

The following is an original article by Dr. Henrietta C. Mears titled "The Bible: Christo-centric." Read it carefully—it packs a lot of punch![1]

The Bible: Christo-centric

There is one principal subject of the Bible to which every other subject is related. The Bible is Christo-centric. Take Christ out of the Old Testament and the whole structure falls apart. The Book, from Genesis to Revelation, has but one theme—*the Bible speaks only of Jesus Christ*. You remember Paul said to the Corinthians, "I determined not to know any thing among you, save Jesus Christ, and Him crucified" (1 Corinthians 2:2). That is the theme of the Bible from beginning to end.

THE KEY THAT UNLOCKS

The subject of the Old Testament is the same as the New. Each complements the other. Neither is complete without the other. They both are "the witness that God has borne concerning His Son" (1 John 5:9, *ASV*). No one can ever understand the Bible unless he sees Christ on every page.[2] He is the One who solves the difficulties in interpretation. He is the key that unlocks every page.

There is a story told of some knights coming to an old castle. The gate was closed and locked. How they wished they could get within the walls, but they could not climb over them. They found a bunch of keys, and eagerly tried each one. How they worked and struggled, but the gate did not respond. Finally, they put in one of the keys, and the great lock came open without the slightest difficulty. Do you suppose those men doubted for a moment that they had found the right key?

This old story reminds us of men going to the Bible. It seems like a Book of Mystery to them. They have tried every key to open it, but every key has failed. The key of man's wisdom has been tried to unlock its treasures, but without success. There is, however, one key that even the humblest can put into the lock, and with Him the gate of understanding opens. Shall we doubt then that Christ is the right key? He is more than the key. He says, "I am the Way, and the Truth" (John 14:6).

THE PICTURE THAT REVEALS

Two little boys were trying to put a puzzle map together. It was a map of the United States. After they had been struggling awhile, one of the little fellows said, "I don't know what a country looks like, but I do know what a man looks like." And so with that they turned it on the other side and with ease put together the face of Abraham Lincoln. It was not hard for them to find where the eye, the ear, the mouth and the forehead went. After it was completed, they turned it over and what do you suppose they found? Yes, the map of the United States.

If you can only find the picture of Christ in the Bible, you will find that the things which seem to puzzle you fit in perfect harmony with the whole. Christ said on one occasion, "Search the Scriptures; for in them ye think ye have eternal life: and they are they which testify of Me" (John 5:39). If we do not find Christ when we study the Scriptures, we study in vain.

ALL TEXTS LEAD TO CHRIST

An old and great minister of the gospel listened to a young minister preach one day. After the sermon the young man, wishing to have the criticism of this experienced older man, asked him what he thought of his sermon.

"Well, now that you ask me, I must tell you that I find one serious fault. There was no Christ in your sermon."

"But," said the young man, "there was no Christ in my text."

"Well," said the elder, "where did you find it?"

"I found it in the Bible, of course."

"Ah," said the old warrior of the faith, "you cannot find a text in the Bible in which there is no Christ. Do you not know, young man, that in England all roads lead to London? And in the Bible every passage points to Calvary?"

"But I do not quite see the way," said the young man.

To this the older man replied, "Then you must find the way, and if you cannot find the way jump over hedges and ditches; but get to Jesus somehow."

A SINGLE THEME

This really is the wonder of the Bible—that it has but one theme and that theme is the Lord Jesus Christ.

If this is so, and Jesus is the subject of the Book, where should we begin? We want to learn all we possibly can about the Lord Jesus Christ, and how shall we commence the study in order that we may? Shall we begin with Genesis and go right through the Book? Some think that if Christ is the main theme of the Bible then we should begin with the Gospels, for they portray His birth, His death and His resurrection. But Matthew begins by saying, "The book of the generation of Jesus Christ, the son of David, the son of Abraham" (Matthew 1:1). He sends you right back to the Old Testament.

Luke goes back further than Matthew, and in giving the genealogy of Jesus Christ he says, "Which was the son of Seth, which was the son of Adam, which was the son of God" (Luke 3:38).

John begins by saying, "In the beginning was the Word, and the Word was with God, and the Word was God" (John 1:1).

Each one of the Gospels takes us back into the Old Testament. Once we know who Christ is from the Gospels, we can go back to the Old Testament and with intelligence and understanding trace His coming into the world. Remember, when Jesus was talking to the men on the way to Emmaus, He began "at Moses and all the prophets," and "expounded unto them in all the scriptures the things concerning Himself" (Luke 24:27, *KJV*).

If we open a novel in the middle and begin to read about the hero, we will soon find that we will have to go back to the beginning and start the book where we should if we are to understand the story, otherwise the plot will be veiled to us. John says, "In the beginning was the Word, and the Word was with God"; then he adds, "all things were made by Him; and without Him was not any thing made that was made" (John 1:1-2). When I turn back to the verse of the first book of the Bible, I read, "In the beginning GOD" (Genesis 1:1), and we see the Creator God who was the Word. We find Jesus in the beginning and all through the book of Genesis.

A VERY INTERESTING THING IS THIS

When you study the Gospels and Acts, in fact any of the Scriptures, you find that the plan of redemption was no afterthought, but it was a clear unfolding of the eternal purpose of God. We read words like this: "The Lamb slain from the foundation of the world" (Revelation 13:8). Can we find anything of this purpose in the Old Testament? If God has a definite idea in mind by which He is to redeem mankind, we cannot help but find Him revealing that purpose. We will see examples in the Old Testament of God working out that principle. Then when the fullness of time was come, God sent His Son into the world to reveal His plan.

We know that it was God's plan to save the world by having His own Son come down to this earth and take upon Himself the form of a man. We call this "the incarnation." This comes from the Latin *in* (meaning "in") and *caro* (meaning "flesh"). Webster says, "the union of Godhead with manhood." God's plan was not to redeem men by giving them a set of rules or by establishing a philosophy of life, but by coming down and being made flesh and living among us.

If it was God's plan to save the world by a personality and that Person was to be His Son, we may expect to see Him puttting His plan in operation from the very beginning of His revelation in the Scriptures. This is just what God does. One of the most interesting and illuminating of all of the studies in the Old Testament is to trace the ancestral line of the Messiah. God reveals everything through His Son. It begins with a promise in Genesis 3:15: "And I will put enmity between thee and the woman, and between thy seed and her seed; it shall bruise thy head, and thou shalt bruise his heel."

SIN DEMANDS A SAVIOUR
It is the fall in the Garden of Eden that makes a Saviour necessary. The fallen race must be lifted up and restored to God. "As in Adam all die, even so in Christ shall all be made alive" (1 Corinthians 15:22). "For as by one man's disobedience many were made sinners, so by the obedience of one shall many be made righteous" (Romans 5:19).

> Love lifted me!
> Love lifted me!
> When nothing else could help,
> Love lifted me!

Christ says that He came to "destroy the works of the devil" (1 John 3:8). It was at the very moment man sinned that God announced His gracious purpose to redeem the world. It is from this promise of the "seed of the woman" that we see the whole plan of God concerning a Saviour unfolding before us. This "seed of woman" (not of man, as in the case of all other men), who was none other than Jesus Christ, should come into the world following a very definite order of events. This is not at all strange, for history rightly interpreted is simply His Story. All history is related to the Lord Jesus Christ, and without human design, all history is dated from His advent into the world; it is either BC or AD.

CHRIST A MEMBER OF OUR RACE
Through the long centuries, God's plan of redemption is expanding from stage to stage. Someone has said that if it were left to man to conceive of a method of redemption, he would have thought of some celestial being, but God says the Saviour of the world is to be "the seed of the woman." This

prophetic statement in Genesis 3:15 does not tell us anything about the nature of His person or work, but these are to appear step by step throughout the coming centuries. We know that He will be a member of our race. "Therefore the Lord Himself shall give you a sign; Behold, a virgin shall conceive, and bear a son, and shall call His name Immanuel" (Isaiah 7:14).

THE STORY OF THE GREATEST HERO

The story of the life of any hero is always fascinating. The Bible relates the most thrilling stories of all literature, and they all lead up to the greatest of all heroes, Jesus Christ. When once you have learned something of the theme of the Bible, which is Jesus Christ, first in the New Testament and discover something of His work and character, then when you go back to the Old Testament, you see Him throwing light on every passage. He will take you by the hand and walk with you all through the Old Testament, as He did those two men on the way to Emmaus, and finally lead you back to the New Testament. Then you will find that it is the very same Jesus who all the prophets had said would come.

Remember, all through this study of the bloodline of the King, that Christ is the center and fulfillment of the promise of "the seed of the woman" from the first man Adam until Jesus is born in Bethlehem, when the fulness of time was come. In Christ's veins ran the royal blood of many great individuals. Of the great number of names given in the genealogy of Jesus Christ, seven are outstanding. Commit these names to your memory in their proper order, and it will give you an outline of the Bible that deals with the 4,000 years of messianic history: Adam, Shem, Abraham, Isaac, Jacob, Judah and David.

The Messiah was to come. God had promised Him. Over and over again He makes a fresh statement of this promise to individuals. The prophets spoke of His coming, and every Jew expected a Messiah. All of these promises and predictions were fulfilled in Christ, the Son of God.

Notes

1. Originally published in *Highlights of Scripture Part One: (A) Through the Bible By Periods and (B) The Blood Line of the Messiah* (Los Angeles, CA: The Gospel Light Press, 1937), pp. 55-61. Note that Dr. Mears used the British spelling for "Saviour" and the masculine pronoun "he" to refer to both men and women. She also apparently quoted Bible passages from memory, and not always word for word. We have added Scripture references where she did not include the verse.
2. Perhaps a bit of hyperbole. Some pages are full of genealogies, and some are tales of woe brought on by sin. The point is that Christ is the main subject of the Bible from the beginning to the end.

TRANSFORMERS
The Mega-story of Human History (Luke 24; Acts 1)

SESSION FOCUS

Jesus' continuing work on the earth as portrayed in the Gospel of Luke and the book of Acts.

KEY VERSES TO MEMORIZE

Wait for the gift my Father promised, which you have heard me speak about. For John baptized with water, but in a few days you will be baptized with the Holy Spirit.

ACTS 1:4-5

WEEKLY READING

DAY 1	Luke 24
DAY 2	Acts 1
DAY 3	John 14
DAY 4	John 15
DAY 5	John 16

FOR LEADERS: SESSION AT A GLANCE

SESSION OUTLINE	60 MIN.	90 MIN.	WHAT YOU WILL DO
Getting started	10	15	Pray and worship
Main points of the chapter	25	35	Discuss how Jesus is God's Word to us
Application and discussion	15	25	Discuss Jesus' ministry of transformation that continues by the Holy Spirit through His followers
Looking ahead	5	5	Prepare for next week
Wrapping up	5	10	Close with prayer or song

The Acts of the Apostles

At its simplest, most basic level, the book of Acts is the history of the birth
and growth of the Church as it was just getting started. The full title of the
book is "Acts of the Apostles." The word "apostles" means "those who are
sent or appointed" and refers to the first leaders in the Jesus movement,
while the word "acts" refers to notable deeds performed by those apostles.
The two lead apostles in the book of Acts are Peter, one of Jesus' original 12
disciples (the one whom Jesus designated to lead the others after He left the
earth), and Paul, a religious leader who at first persecuted followers of Christ
but who later became one of the greatest proponents in the Jesus movement.

The book begins in Jerusalem with the resurrected Jesus giving His final instructions to His disciples and then ascending into heaven. It ends
in Rome with the apostle Paul under house arrest but preaching the gospel
relatively unhindered. It spans a little more than 30 years, from Jesus' resurrection and ascension (the spring of AD 32) until three years before the
death of the apostle Paul (about AD 67). Scripture does not tell us about
Paul's death, but we know from Eusebius (AD 263–339), a court historian
for the Roman Emperor Constantine who wrote sometime after AD 320,
that Emperor Nero had Paul beheaded in Rome. This sad event likely occurred during the winter of AD 67.

TRANSFORMERS, PARTS I AND 2

Lots of movies have sequels. For example, the movie *Transformers* had a se-
quel called *Transformers: Revenge of the Fallen*. Similarly, Acts is part of a
larger story that began with the Gospel of Luke and, like the two movies
mentioned, Luke and Acts are about transformers—just different kinds.

According to Eusebius and Irenaeus (c. AD 180), Early Church Fathers,
the author of both books is Luke. (Incidentally, the authors of the Gospels
didn't name themselves out of modesty, not because they were trying to
hide something—we know their names from post-New Testament Christian writers.) "Luke" is a Greek name, not a Jewish name, and based on
this and the fact that Luke is intensely alert to Gentile sensibilities in both
books, we can surmise that he was a Gentile believer in Jesus who wanted
to communicate well to other Gentiles. Luke is known as "the beloved
physician" (Colossians 4:14, *KJV*) and was Paul's traveling companion during some of Paul's missionary journeys (as seen by the shift from "they" to
"we" in Acts 16:6-17; 20:5-21:18; 27:1-28:16). He was also a close atten-
dant near the end of Paul's life (see 2 Timothy 4:11).

Both Luke and Acts start with similar remarks from the author (see Luke 1:1-4; Acts 1:1-2). In Luke's Gospel, he describes that work as a thorough research project; in Acts, he refers back to that book as "my former book." Both are addressed to the same person, Theophilus, a Greek name meaning "friend of God." Scholars are unsure as to whether this refers to an actual person or is an honorary title, but in either case, Luke's purpose in writing his Gospel and Acts is to present an "orderly account" so believers "may know the certainty of the things" they have been taught (Luke 1:3-4). In presenting both the ministry of Jesus in the Gospel of Luke and the beginning of the Church in Acts, Luke shows believers that the foundation of their faith is secure.

Many scholars believe the Gospel of Luke was written before AD 70, which would place the writing of Acts at around the same time.[1] There are several reasons for this dating. First, there is no reference in Luke to the fall of Jerusalem to the Roman Emperor Titus in AD 70, which was a significant event for both Jews and Christians and one that Luke would have certainly included. Second, as previously noted, Luke makes no mention of the death of Paul, which occurred around AD 67. Third, Luke wrote Acts as a historian interpreting events that occurred at an earlier time, though it is apparent he took part in many of the episodes.[2] Even more striking is the fact that Luke appears to have not read the letters of Paul, which makes a later dating of the book less likely.

A QUESTION ON HISTORICAL ACCURACY

As a historian, Luke is not without his critics. Many scholars have accused Luke of sacrificing historical accuracy for the sake of his theological perspective—of altering events and "rewriting" the history of the early Jesus movement to make certain doctrinal points.[3] Much of this criticism comes from what some see as contradictions between Luke's account of the apostle Paul in Acts and Paul's own writings.[4]

One of the main problems in determining Luke's historical accuracy is the difficulty in knowing what sources he used in his writings. We know from Luke's Gospel that both he and Matthew drew on Mark's Gospel, but Luke also drew on secondary sources (known only as the "Q" document, short for German *Quelle* or "source"), which were likely personal conversations with prominent members in the early Jesus movement. If those individuals provided erroneous information—or if Luke truly altered what he had heard to fit a specific agenda—it would call into question the historical accuracy of both the Gospel of Luke and the book of Acts.

There are a few points to keep in mind when considering these claims. First, there is no evidence that either Luke or those in the early Jesus movement were driven solely by theology and not interested in the history of the movement. "Belief" and "history" are not exclusive—and Luke states up front that his desire is to set down an *accurate* account of Jesus' ministry and the early followers of Christ. In fact, scholars have found that Luke is quite accurate in his portrayal of first-century Roman life—archaeologists have proven that the details he provides about names, titles, customs and practices in different places are correct. In this way, the events Luke reports *support* his theology, rather than the other way around.

But what about the accuracy of Luke's sources? While it is impossible to identify each individual account Luke uses (he was skillful in blending them into a cohesive narrative), there is evidence to show that these sources were reliable. According to Colossians 4:10,14, Luke was with John Mark (the author of the Gospel) when Paul wrote that letter, which would have given him access to information about the early growth of the Church. Luke tells us in Acts 12:12 of a prayer meeting held in the home of Mark's mother, which would have allowed Luke to speak with other leaders in the Jesus movement.[5] In addition, scholars have argued that churches were faithful in preserving the early traditions of how their congregations were established and the activities of the apostles.[6] Based on this evidence, Scottish archaeologist and New Testament scholar William Ramsay noted, "Luke is a historian of the first rank [and] should be placed along with the very greatest of historians."[7]

Luke's Purpose for Writing the Book of Acts

At the beginning of Acts, Luke states, "In my former book [the Gospel of Luke] . . . I wrote about all that Jesus began to do and to teach" (1:1). An unspoken but clear implication here is that Jesus didn't ever stop *doing* and *teaching*. Therefore, the book of Acts will be about all that Jesus *continued* to do and teach after He rose from the grave and ascended into heaven.

In this way, the end of the Gospel of Luke and the beginning of Acts overlap one another, indicating how Jesus continues to act in the world. Luke's Gospel finishes with God raising Jesus from the dead, several post-resurrection appearances, Jesus authorizing His disciples to preach the gospel to all nations, Jesus telling the disciples to wait for the promise of the Father, and Jesus' ascension into heaven (see Luke 24). Acts begins by acknowledging 40 days of Jesus' post-resurrection appearances (see Acts 1:3); Jesus authorizing His disciples to preach the gospel everywhere, even to the ends of the earth (see 1:8); Jesus' order for His disciples to stay in Jerusalem and wait for the gift God had promised (1:4); and Jesus' ascension into heaven (see 1:9).

In overlapping these events, Luke emphasizes the centrality of the resurrection of Jesus, His ascension into heaven, and the giving of the promise of the Father—the precious Holy Spirit—to the Church. Jesus didn't just rise from the dead, prove Himself risen, and then disappear. Instead, He ascended to the right hand of the Father, and from there He reigns as the risen Lord of history (see 1 Peter 3:21-22). From this heavenly throne, God the Father and God the Son send forth God the Holy Spirit upon the believers in Acts (see John 14:26; 15:26). In many ways, the Acts of the Apostles could legitimately be called the "Acts of the Holy Spirit," because none of the supernatural deeds the apostles accomplish happen apart from the work of the Spirit.

In the Gospel of Luke, the chief transformer is Jesus. Filled with the Holy Spirit, Jesus transforms the world with His life, deeds, teaching, death and resurrection. In Acts, the chief transformer is still Jesus, but this time Jesus works through His people who are filled, motivated, animated, guided and empowered by the Holy Spirit. The book of Acts does not end with the disciples and the first believers—as inheritors of their legacy, we also are "Jesus People." Jesus transforms us by the Holy Spirit, and we then transform our families, churches, communities and world into something that more closely resembles God's intentions for us.

Mega-story: The Center of Human History

Luke's Gospel and the book of Acts mirror each other in other ways, which serves to reinforce the unity of the entire narrative. Luke recounts the ministry of Jesus the Messiah in His role as servant, while Acts recounts the continuation of Jesus' ministry via His role as risen Lord. Both books center all of human history on Jesus' life, deeds, death, resurrection and ascension.

Together, both Luke and Acts teach that the gospel is a universal message that applies to all people and all cultures. Luke's Gospel first acknowledges the world's rulers (see 1:52); traces Jesus' genealogy all the way back to Adam (see 3:38); follows Jesus around in His Galilean, Judean and

Samarian ministries (see 4–19); and then focuses Jesus' later ministry, including His death and resurrection in and around Jerusalem (see 20–24).

Reversing direction, the book of Acts starts narrowly and then widens to the whole world. First, the risen Lord commands His followers to be His witnesses in Jerusalem, Judea and Samaria and to the ends of the earth (see 1:8). The rest of the book then follows the gospel's progress from Jerusalem (see 1–7); to Judea, Galilee, Samaria and Ethiopia (see 8–12); and then to Asia Minor (what is now Turkey), Macedonia and Greece (see 13–20). Finally, Acts covers the journey of Paul to Rome, the symbol of Gentile kingdoms and of the ends of the earth (see 21–28).

Luke's literary pattern in his Gospel and Acts—of starting big; narrowing to Jesus' cross, resurrection and ascension in Jerusalem; and then widening again to embrace the whole earth—serves to underscore the centrality of Jesus in human history. Luke and Acts teach us that Jesus is not just the Jewish Messiah but also Lord and Savior of all peoples.

God's Sovereignty

Another of the major themes in both Luke and Acts is God's sovereignty—the idea that God's plan cannot be thwarted. God is always working behind the scenes to bring about His purposes. This theme comes across in Luke and Acts in many ways:

- Fulfillment of prophecy is a prominent theme in both books. History is moving inexorably toward God's ultimate purposes.

- In both Luke and Acts, prayer is an important means of discovering God's sovereign will, bringing it out into the open and living it out.

- God's protection is a big theme in both books. In Luke 4:28-30, God protects Jesus from the angry mob; in Acts 14:19, He protects Paul from death by stoning.

- In Luke, Jesus said that whoever wanted to follow Him must be willing to publicly identify with Him, "take up their cross," and risk humiliating death (see 9:23; 14:27). This happened again and again in the book of Acts. The very word we translate as "witnesses" in Acts 1:8 is *marturoi* (the plural of *martus*), from which we get the word "martyrs." The apostles were arrested and beaten (see 5:17-41); Stephen was stoned to death (see 7:54-60); the believers were run out of Jerusalem (see 8:1-4); Paul arrested believers and put them to death (see 9:1-2); and King Herod had the apostle James killed (see 12:2). And yet, because Jesus' followers believed God was in control, they could rejoice and worship God despite the persecution (see 5:41; 16:25).

• God gives supernatural guidance and communication through angels (24 times in Luke and 22 times in Acts).

• The Holy Spirit plays an important role in the Gospel of Luke (He is mentioned 17 times) and an even more visible role in Acts (He is mentioned 56 times).

• In Luke's Gospel, Jesus promises that when His followers are brought before human judges and tribunals, the Holy Spirit will give them the words they need (see 12:11-12; 21:12-15). In Acts, this is exactly what happens. A great deal of emphasis is placed on the Spirit-inspired speeches of Peter (see 2:14; 3:12; 4:8), Stephen (see 6:15; 7:1-2), and Paul (see 13:16; 17:22; 19:30; 21:40; 23:1,6; 24:10,24-25; 25:8; 26:1; 28:17,25).

• Prayer is another prominent theme in Luke and Acts, and one that we will return to again in later sessions. For now, note that the book of Acts begins with the disciples, including women, going into an upstairs room where they are constantly praying and waiting for the promise of the Father (the Holy Spirit) that Jesus had told them about (see 1:12-14). These disciples didn't passively wait; they intensively and actively waited, together, with great anticipation.

Another example of God's sovereignty is the Matthias incident. In the Gospel of Luke, Jesus had selected 12 disciples, but Judas had betrayed Him. In Acts 1:15-26, citing two prophecies in the book of Psalms (69:25 and 109:8), the 11 remaining disciples feel compelled to find a replacement for Judas. Without waiting for the "promise of the Father" to send the Holy Spirit, they move forward with their plan to replace Judas, pray for God's will to be done, and cast lots.

Casting lots is like tossing a coin or throwing dice. Today, many of us follow this same model—we use common sense and human wisdom when facing tough decisions, in effect leaving things up to chance. However, our ways are not necessarily God's ways (see Isaiah 55:8), even if we are sincere believers in Jesus and are praying for lots to decide a matter. In this case, the lots fell to Matthias, and he was thereafter counted as among "the apostles" (see 1:27) and "the Eleven" (see 2:14).

This is the last time we hear of lots being cast in the book of Acts. After God pours His Spirit out on the Church in Acts 2, He provides supernatural guidance to His people through angels and the Holy Spirit. One highlight of this supernatural guidance is that the risen Jesus reveals Himself personally to Paul and chooses him to be an apostle to the Gentiles (see Acts 9:15-16; 22:14-15; 26:16-18; Galatians 2:8; 1 Timothy 2:7). Paul then becomes the lead character of the second half of Acts (as well as the author of much of the New Testament). In effect, Jesus chooses Paul—in addition to Matthias—to "take the place" of the missing Judas. In this way, God's sovereignty goes beyond the old way of making a decision.

Jews for Jesus!

Like any good story, Acts has a central conflict. In this case, the conflict is both cultural and spiritual in nature. The Church began as a Jewish Jesus movement. Almost all the earliest followers of Jesus had grown up Jewish and were trying to maintain their traditions despite living under Roman rule. For them, Jesus was the Messiah promised by their Holy Scriptures, the end-time king appointed and approved by God. Now that Jesus had died on the cross and God had raised Him from the dead, what was next?

The early believers in Christ had to grapple with a number of unanswered questions. One was what the relationship should be between the Jews who believed in Jesus and their fellow Jews who did not. Should the Jewish believers continue to attend synagogue worship services on "the day of rest," the Sabbath (Saturday)? Or should they worship on "the Lord's day," the day of Jesus' resurrection (Sunday)? Or should they try to steer a middle course?

Another question was whether Jesus, the Messiah of God, would come back immediately to the earth and establish peace, righteousness and the blessings of God's kingdom—with the kings of the earth submitting to Him as promised in Scripture. If there was to be some delay in the full coming of God's Messianic kingdom on the earth, what character would the new Jewish Jesus movement take? In particular, what should be done about the Gentiles (Hebrew *goyyim*), the non-Jewish peoples and nations on the earth? From a Jewish perspective, the Gentiles had lived religiously and morally impure lives. If they now accepted Christ, how could they ever be made pure enough to be included in the Church? Wouldn't it be better for the Gentiles to convert to Judaism first and start living under the laws of Moses?

Another question centered on what course to take if persecution were to arise from their own religious community or from unbelieving Gentiles. Should they fight back? Or should they just allow events to transpire? In addition, what kinds of communities were believers in Jesus to exhibit? Were there to be new models of relationships that the Jesus People were to implement—not only in their personal relationships but also in the world?

All of these questions are churning beneath the surface of the narrative in Acts. It is these questions that motivate the main characters in the story to act in the way they do, and ultimately these issues that determine the structure of the early Jesus movement. We will return to these questions as we move through the story, examining how God directed events and accomplished His will through the lives of His followers.

QUESTIONS FOR PERSONAL APPLICATION AND DISCUSSION

Each of the activities below is appropriate for personal study. These activities are also suitable as prompts for small-group discussion.

What evidence do we have that both the Gospel of Luke and Acts were written by the same author? What does Luke's name tell us about who he was and the audience to which he was writing?

_____

_____

_____

_____

_____

What are some of the criticisms leveled at Luke's Gospel and the book of
Acts? What are some reasons for believing Luke is an accurate historian?

_____

_____

_____

_____

Read Luke 24:45-53 and Acts 1:1-11. What are some of the similarities and
differences between the two accounts?

_____

_____

_____

_____

In what ways do Luke and Acts show that the gospel is a universal message
for all peoples and all cultures?

_____

_____

_____

_____

In the Gospel of Luke, a central part of Jesus' ministry was preaching and
demonstrating to His disciples that the kingdom of God had arrived. Read
the following verses in Acts and note how the early leaders in the Church
carried on Jesus' teachings about the kingdom of God.

PASSAGE	HOW THE EARLY LEADERS CARRIED ON JESUS' TEACHINGS
Acts 8:12	
Acts 14:21-22	
Acts 19:8	
Acts 20:17-25	
Acts 28:23	

Read Acts 1:15-26. How did the 11 disciples decide who should replace Judas? What was their basis for doing this? What was the result? Why don't we see them repeating this practice again in the book of Acts?

_____

_____

_____

_____

Read Luke 3:15-17 and review Acts 1:4-5. What did John prophesy would come after Him? How was that fulfilled in the Gospel of Luke? How was it fulfilled in the book of Acts?

_____

_____

_____

_____

Luke briefly mentions "the promise of the Father" in Luke 24:49 and Acts 1:4. A more extended discussion on this topic can be found in John 14–16. Review John 14:15-31 and John 16:5-16. What did Jesus say specifically in these passages about the Holy Spirit—the Counselor and the Spirit of Truth? What did Jesus mean when He said, "It is for your good that I am going away" (John 16:7)?

_____

_____

_____

_____

The disciples were told to wait for the promise of the Father, who would be given in a few days. "Waiting for" or "waiting on" the Lord is something the Old Testament encourages. Look up the following passages and note what each says about the benefits of waiting for God to act.

PASSAGE	THE BENEFITS OF WAITING ON THE LORD
Psalm 27:14	
Psalm 37:7-9	

PASSAGE	THE BENEFITS OF WAITING ON THE LORD
Isaiah 25:9	
Isaiah 40:31	
Micah 7:7	

For us, the Holy Spirit has already been given to the Church. Yet how might waiting for the Lord (and the Holy Spirit) still apply?

_____

_____

_____

Notes

1. Other scholars date Luke and Acts from AD 90–100. It has even been suggested that Luke wrote Acts before his Gospel. See C.S.C. Williams, *A Commentary on the Acts of the Apostles* (London, UK: Adam & Charles Black, 1978).
2. Some have suggested that the use of "we" in the later chapters in Acts is a literary device that Luke used to show he was an experienced traveler and thus a competent writer (see I. Howard Marshall, *Luke: Historian and Theologian* [Downer's Grove, IL: InterVarsity Press, 1988]). The more plausible explanation is that Luke witnessed these events, and this is how Luke's original readers would have interpreted the shift in style.
3. A similar charge has been leveled against Matthew's Gospel, especially in his story of the massacre of the innocents (see Matthew 2:16-18), as the Jewish historian Flavius Josephus did not record the event in any of his writings. See Michael Grant, *Herod the Great* (Durrington, UK: Littlehampton Book Services, 1971).
4. Some of these include: (1) Luke's portrayal of Paul as a pious observer of the Law (see Acts 16:3; 21:18-26; 26:5; compare with Paul's words in 1 Corinthians 9:19-23; Galatians 2:5,11); (2) Luke's depiction of Paul being brought into the Jerusalem church and his close association with the apostles after his conversion (see Acts 9:10-19,23-30; compare with Galatians 1:15-24); and (3) Luke's apparent "refusal" to depict Paul as an apostle (compare with Galatians 1:1). None of these are really contradictions: (1) Luke shows Paul's willingness to live as a Jew among Jews but does not imply that this "bound" him or his Gentile converts in any way; (2) Luke never lays out a specific timetable but just states "after many days" (Acts 9:23), which could comprise three years; and (3) Acts 14:4,14 reveals that Luke knew Paul was an apostle.
5. See Donald Guthrie, *New Testament Introduction* (Downer's Grove, IL: InterVarsity Press, 1990).
6. See Jacob Jervell, *Luke and the People of God: A New Look at Luke-Acts* (Minneapolis, MN: Augsburg Publishing House, 1972).
7. William Ramsay, *The Bearing of Recent Discovery on the Trustworthiness of the New Testament* (London: Hodder & Stoughton, 1915).

Sources

I. Howard Marshall, *The Acts of the Apostles: An Introduction and Commentary*, Tyndale New Testament Commentaries (Grand Rapids, MI: William B. Eerdmans, 1989), pp. 34-44.
Henrietta C. Mears, *What the Bible Is All About*, "Understanding Acts" (Ventura, CA: Regal Books, 2011), chapter 31.

A SHADOWY STAR
The Holy Spirit in the Bible

SESSION FOCUS

The Holy Spirit has been present and active since the time of creation.

KEY VERSE TO MEMORIZE

"Not by might nor by power, but by my Spirit," says the LORD Almighty.
ZECHARIAH 4:6

WEEKLY READING

DAY 1	Genesis 1:2; 41:1-40; Exodus 31:1-11; 35:30-35; Numbers 24:1-14
DAY 2	Judges 3:7-11; 6:33-35; 11:29-33; 14:1-7; 15:1-15
DAY 3	1 Samuel 10:9-13; 11:1-6; 16:14-23; 19:18-24
DAY 4	Ezekiel 1; 9:1-4; 10:15-22; 11:16-24; 43:1-5; 44:1-4
DAY 5	Romans 8:1-11,22-27; Ephesians 5:15-21; 2 Thessalonians 2:13-17; 1 Peter 1:1-12; 2 Peter 1:19-21; Revelation 22:7-21

FOR LEADERS: SESSION AT A GLANCE

SESSION OUTLINE	60 MIN.	90 MIN.	WHAT YOU WILL DO
Getting started	10	15	Pray and worship
Main points of the chapter	25	35	Discuss how Jesus is God's Word to us
Application and discussion	15	25	Discuss the role of the Holy Spirit in biblical history and in our lives
	5	5	
Looking ahead	5	10	Prepare for next week
Wrapping up			Close with prayer or song

The Star of the Show

In the previous session, we saw that the Holy Spirit is the central player—the actual "star of the show"—in the book of Acts. We also noted that another name for the book could be the "Acts of the Holy Spirit." But who *is* the Holy Spirit? What does He do? What sort of relationship should we seek to cultivate with Him, and how can we do that? These questions are the focus of this session, and in answering them we will take a look at the role of the Holy Spirit in both the Old and New Testaments.

SKITTISH ABOUT THE SPIRIT

Before proceeding any further, it is important to acknowledge that for many people, the Holy Spirit is something of an enigmatic and shadowy figure. Even the mention of the name "Holy Spirit" gives them the willies.

Part of the problem might be caused by the people they see on television who talk a lot about the Holy Spirit and seem odd or downright strange to them. Or perhaps the problem may be caused by fear of deception—with "reality" shows lumping poltergeists, alien abductions and faith healings into one "spiritual" basket, it's often easy to blur the line between what's real and what's fake. People don't want to be taken in and fooled.

Yet another part of the problem may be the phrase "the Holy Ghost," which is the term used in the *King James Version* of the Bible. It survives in church hymns such as "Praise God, from Whom All Blessings Flow":

Praise God, from Whom all blessings flow;
Praise Him, all creatures here below;
Praise Him above, ye heavenly host;
Praise Father, Son, and Holy Ghost.

This phrase may have communicated well to people 400 years ago, but the word "ghost" today creates childish, cartoonish ideas about the Holy Spirit in many people's minds. Still another part of the problem may be peer pressure. In some circles, belief in non-physical spirits of any kind is considered hopelessly old-fashioned, unscientific, superstitious and unbelievable. Why even go there?

Finally, in many churches there is a lack of good teaching on the Holy Spirit. This session is about dispelling some of the shadows and fog surrounding the Holy Spirit.

A RELUCTANT STAR

As we begin our task, immediately we face the irony that though the Holy Spirit is a major figure in the Bible, He is actually quite modest. The Holy Spirit generally prefers to avoid a lot of attention and to orchestrate things from behind the scenes. Like an expert stage hand, He throws the spotlight on God and Jesus Christ. However, this doesn't mean that the Holy Spirit isn't present throughout the Bible. In fact, we encounter Him from the very first pages clear through to the end.

Before we begin to examine how the Holy Spirit fits into the larger story of the entire Bible, it is important to remember two helpful rules of the road for doing Bible study. The first is the "rule of first mention." This rule states that the first mention of a word or phrase in the Bible can yield powerful insights into the significance of the term throughout the whole Bible. This rule is not absolute—sometimes key meanings do not appear the first time they are mentioned—but it often works quite well.

A second rule, and one we always want to consider, is the context in which the word or phrase appears. Context comes in three expanding circles: (1) the immediate circle of sentences, paragraphs and book in which the phrase is found; (2) the intermediate circle of the type of writing—such as history, poetry, proverb or prophecy—in which the phrase is found; and (3) the wider circle of how the phrase fits into the overall revelation of God in Scripture. To apply the contextual principle well, it is important to also be somewhat aware of how modern times and culture are different from the times and cultures of the Bible.

The Holy Spirit in Scripture

The Old Testament writings, composed over a period of about 1,400 years, were collected together approximately 400 years before Jesus Christ. They represent the old covenant (or promise or agreement) that God had with His people. In the early stages of the Old Testament, God's people are called the "Hebrews"; later, they are known as the "Israelites"; and finally, they are referred to as the "Jews." The Old Testament writings look forward to and anticipate a coming Messiah or King.

The New Testament was written after Jesus' death and resurrection. Composed over a period of approximately 50 to 60 years, they look back on Jesus' life, deeds and teachings; His death and resurrection; and the formation of His followers into the early Jesus movment. It is important to remember that while the *same* Holy Spirit is present in both Testaments, there are some differences in how the Holy Spirit is portrayed.

THE HOLY SPIRIT AS "BREATH OF GOD"

Applying the first-mention rule, we find that the Holy Spirit first appears in the second verse of the Bible (Genesis 1:2): "Now the earth was formless and empty, darkness was over the surface of the deep, and the Spirit of God [Hebrew *Ruach Elohim*] was hovering over the waters."

Hebrew is a richly metaphorical language, and *Ruach Elohim* is a richly evocative phrase. *Elohim* is the main word for God in the Hebrew Bible and is used more than 2,300 times. *Ruach* literally means "breath." If you are experiencing someone else's breath, you are very close to that person—that person is alive and present to you. The imagery in the phrase *Ruach Elohim* indicates that God is not an abstract principle or a mere impersonal force, but that through His Spirit He is passionately alive, personal, present and close to His people.

Maybe you've heard or sung the hymn "Breathe on Me, Breath of God." The breath of God in our lives is refreshing, renewing, invigorating and inspiring. It awakens us to what God is doing and what God wants us to do.

THE HOLY SPIRIT AS PART OF THE TRINITY

The *immediate* context of Genesis 1:2 is found in Genesis 1:1: "In the beginning God created the heavens and the earth." Here, the Holy Spirit is an active player in creation, not a passive wallflower. Also active in creation is the Word of God (see Genesis 1:3,6,9,11,14,20,24,26,29), through whom God creates everything by speaking it into existence. The New Testament identifies this Word as God the Son (see John 1:1-3,14). In short, we owe our existence to God the Father, God the Spirit, and God the Word. Our purpose as humans is to reflect God's image in the world (see Genesis 1:26-27).

The *intermediate* context is that the book of Genesis, in which the term *Ruach Elohim* is first found, is a story of beginnings. We have the magnificent and miraculous story of creation, the first humans, the first sin, God's first promises, the first murder, the first mega-city and the first (the founding) fathers of the faith: Abraham, Isaac and Jacob.

In the *wider circle* of the whole Bible, Genesis 1:1-3 tells us that God is magnificent, powerful, endlessly creative and concerned for His creation. God is One; but within His Oneness, the Spirit and the Word lend a dynamism, energy, friendship and intimacy within God. The Church would later vividly describe this dynamism and intimacy within God as *perichoreuein,* or the "divine dance." The biblical picture that emerges is not God-as-essence or God-as-static-figurehead but God-as-relational. There is diversity yet unity within God. In the gospel, He is inviting us into an intimate friendship (and "dance") that has existed for all eternity.

This relational aspect of God has tremendous implications for the rest of the Bible and for all of our relationships. The problem of sin is essentially relational between us and God. The problems between humans are relational. In Christ, God-the-Word became a man to reconcile us to God and to restore our broken relationships in society. The Holy Spirit changes our hearts and activates our desires so that we want to have a "vertical" love relationship with God and express that love relationship in our "horizontal" relationships with other human beings.

THE HOLY SPIRIT'S PRESENCE IN PEOPLE

The Holy Spirit appears in other key passages of the Old Testament. In Genesis 41:38, Joseph, a Hebrew slave fresh from Pharaoh's prison, has just interpreted Pharoah's dream and told Pharaoh how to prepare for the coming seven good years and seven bad years depicted in the dream. Pharaoh turns to his courtiers and says, in effect, "Can we find anyone else like this fellow who has the Spirit of God in him?" This shows that God's Holy Spirit, the Spirit of the Lord, can be "in" or "on" a person in such a way that the person exhibits prophetic insight and exceptional wisdom.

In Exodus 31:3, God tells Moses that He has filled Bazalel with the Spirit of God so that he can create works of art in silver, bronze, gold, wood, stones and all kinds of crafts. These artistic works were to be used in the construction of the moveable worship tent, the Tabernacle. God is not against art! He affirms beauty, art and the creative arts. They reflect God's glory and are good gifts.

In Numbers 11:25, in a one-time event, the presence of the Lord in the form of a cloud comes upon Moses, and Moses then parcels out some of the power of the Holy Spirit on 70 elders of Israel. The Holy Spirit "rests" on them so they prophesy, but it doesn't happen again. Moses then says, "I wish that all the LORD's people were prophets and that the LORD would put his Spirit on them!" (verse 29). This didn't occur during Old Testament times; Moses' wish is an aspiration pointing forward to what will happen in Acts 2.

In Numbers 24, the Spirit of God comes upon Balaam, the psychic-for-hire whom Balak, the king of Moab, had hired to curse Israel. Balaam is an odd character. He may have had a legitimate gift from God, but he misused his gift and led many people away from God, and his prophetic career ended in disgrace. However, in this instance God actually speaks to Balaam, and Balaam ends up prophesying good for the Israelites instead of cursing them. This story is an example of God getting the last laugh: He reaffirms His promises to Israel and at the same time overturns Balak's scheme to destroy Israel.

In the book of Judges, the Spirit of the Lord powerfully comes upon individuals who then carry out God's will (see 3:10; 6:34; 11:29; 13:25; 14:6,9; 15:14).

THE HOLY SPIRIT AS GOD'S SHEKINAH GLORY

In the Old Testament, God's glory, God's dwelling place and God's Spirit are ideas that work together. God wanted to create a people for Himself—a people in whom He could dwell and in whom He could express His glory. God begins to form this people in the book of Genesis, but it isn't until the book of Exodus that they truly come together to form a nation. In Exodus, God frees His people from bondage to the Egyptians through a series of amazing miracles (signs and wonders).

In Exodus 15, after the people have been redeemed from slavery in Egypt, they excitedly celebrate with a victory song, proclaiming, "Who among the gods is like you, LORD? Who is like you—majestic in holiness, awesome in glory, working wonders?" (verse 11). They acknowledge God's unfailing love and that He wants to guide them to His holy dwelling place (see verse 13), where God's glory, through His Spirit, will dwell.

However, something that will leave a lasting impression on the people must happen first. Before God's dwelling place can be esablished, He needs to reveal His will through the giving of the Law. So, the people find themselves at the base of Mount Sinai, the Mountain of God. The mountain is covered with dark smoke, it's spewing forth fire, it's quaking and shaking, and what seems like a trumpet blast is getting louder and louder. God warns the people to stay back or they will die (see Exodus 19:16-19). The people, including Moses, are shaking with fear. Only then does God give Moses the Ten Commandments (see 20:1-21). So, in the escape from Egypt and in the giving of the Law, God reveals His glory to His people.

Only after the importance of the Ten Commandments is established does God allow Moses to turn his attention to the building of the Tabernacle (see Exodus 24–40), the moveable worship tent that would be the dwelling place of the Lord. There, the Shekinah glory—the active, awesome presence of God through His Spirit—would dwell. Finally, at the end of the book of Exodus, the glory of the Lord spectacularly fills the Tabernacle (see 40:34-35).

The Movements of God's Shekinah Glory

The humble, moveable Tabernacle tent was a foretaste of the permanent, awesome Temple that Solomon would build in Jerusalem. Just as God had filled the Tabernacle with His Shekinah glory, He graciously filled Solomon's Temple as well (see 2 Chronicles 7:1-3). However, Israel sinned against God again and again and stubbornly insisted on worshiping Him not as the supreme king of the universe, but as one god among many. Israel wanted to mix and match worship of God with worship of the gods of the surrounding peoples. As a result, and after many warnings, God had enough.

The book of Ezekiel gives the fateful consequences. It opens with the prophet's vision of the glory of God (see Ezekiel 1). From that point on until Ezekiel 40, the prophet describes an unbearably sad progression of events. The glory of the God of Israel moves from the holiest place in the Temple (see 9:3), then to the Temple's threshhold (see 10:4), then departs the Temple and rises above it (see 10:18), and then flits from the walls of the city to the mountain on the east side of the city, finally departing to Babylonia (see 11:23-24).

Following this, in one of the most poignant passages in the Bible, Ezekiel envisions a restored Temple at the end of time. The glory of the Lord returns to the Temple from the east, whence it had previously departed, and fills it as before (see 43:2-5; 44:4). The New Testament sees Acts 2, the coming of the Holy Spirit on Jesus' followers in the "last days" after His resurrection, as the fulfillment of this prophecy. As the apostle Paul says, "Don't you know that you yourselves are God's temple and that God's Spirit dwells in your midst?" (1 Corinthians 3:16; see also 6:19). From that point on, God's Shekinah glory would dwell not in the Temple or some other location but within the followers of Christ themselves. The Church had been born.

QUESTIONS FOR PERSONAL APPLICATION AND DISCUSSION

What are your feelings about the Holy Spirit? Do you understand His role in the Trinity, or does He seem a bit obscure to you? How has this session helped your understanding?

_____

_____

_____

_____

What does the term _Ruach Elohim_ in Genesis 1:2 indicate about the character of the Holy Spirit? Why is it important that He is mentioned at this place in the Bible?

_____

_____

_____

_____

How does the image of the Trinity reveal the relational aspect of God? In what ways does this have tremendous impact on our relationship with God and others?

_____

_____

_____

_____

In the Old Testament, where does the Shekinah glory of God initially dwell? What happens during the course of Israel's history to shift God's presence from the land? What did Ezekiel prophesy would occur at the end of time?

_____

_____

_____

_____

_____

The Old Testament Hebrew poets (such as King David) would create rhymes with ideas. They would use the rhymes as two ways of describing the same thing. Look at Psalm 51:11 and Psalm 139:7. What two ideas are parallel to each other here? What does this tell you about the Holy Spirit?

_____

_____

_____

_____

_____

The Holy Spirit is never portrayed in the Bible as an impersonal force. Look up the following passages from the Old and New Testaments and write down how they indicate the Holy Spirit is personally involved in our lives in a relational way.

Old Testament Passage	New Testament Passage	What These Tell Us About How the Holy Spirit Is Involved in Our Lives
Isaiah 63:10	Ephesians 4:30	
Ezekiel 36:26	John 3:5-8	
Judges 15:14	Acts 1:8	

Read John 7:37-39 and Numbers 20:1-5. In the passage in John, Jesus was in Jerusalem for the Feast of Tabernacles (also known as the Feast of Booths), a festival commemorating the autumn harvest and the Israelites' wandering in the wilderness. The Jews would "camp out" and re-create some of the hardships of their ancestors' journey. Why would Jesus' words have particularly resonated with them at this time?

_____

_____

_____

_____

Jesus' invitation is based in passages from the Old Testament that would
have been familiar to His Jewish listeners. Read Isaiah 44:3 and 55:1. What
themes are present in each of these verses?

_____

_____

_____

_____

_____

In John 7:39, we read that when Jesus spoke of "living water," He meant the
Holy Spirit "whom those who believed in him were later to receive." John
adds that up to that time the Holy Spirit had not been given, because Jesus had not yet been "glorified." What do you think John meant by this?
(Hint: Read Acts 2:33.)

_____

_____

_____

_____

_____

Is the Holy Spirit as accessible to us as in the days of the early Jesus movement? How important is it to have the Holy Spirit within us to follow Jesus and live a life that is pleasing to God?

_____

_____

_____

_____

_____

Sources
Henrietta C. Mears, *What the Bible Is All About,* "Understanding Acts" (Ventura, CA: Regal Books, 2011),
    chapter 31.
Mears, *Highlights of Scripture, Part Four: Words and Works of Jesus, Teacher's Book* (Los Angeles, CA: The
    Gospel Light Press, 1937).

HAPPY BIRTHDAY, CHURCH
Baptism by Fire (Acts 2)

SESSION FOCUS

The events of Acts take place in a Jewish setting and fulfill
Old Testament prophecies.

KEY VERSE TO MEMORIZE

But you will receive power when the Holy Spirit comes on you;
and you will be my witnesses in Jerusalem, and in all Judea and Samaria,
and to the ends of the earth.
ACTS 1:8

WEEKLY READING

DAY 1	Exodus 12–14
DAY 2	Exodus 19–20
DAY 3	2 Chronicles 7:1-3; Isaiah 40:3-5; 60:1-2,19; Ezekiel 44:4
DAY 4	Acts 2
DAY 5	Psalms 16; 110; Joel 2:28-32

FOR LEADERS: SESSION AT A GLANCE

SESSION OUTLINE	60 MIN.	90 MIN.	WHAT YOU WILL DO
Getting started	10	15	Pray and worship
Main points of the chapter	25	35	Discuss how Jesus is God's Word to us
Application and discussion	15	25	Discuss how Jesus baptizes us with the Holy Spirit and with power, fulfilling God's promises in Scripture
Looking ahead	5	5	Prepare for next week
Wrapping up	5	10	Close with prayer or song

A Jewish Setting

Christians often forget that Jesus was thoroughly Jewish. He grew up an observant Jew. He prayed to the God of Abraham, Isaac and Jacob. He and His family went to the local synogogue on the Sabbath (Saturday), the Jewish day of worship. As required by Jewish law, He and His family also visited the Temple in Jerusalem for the seasonal religious festivals. When He started His public ministry, He quoted prophecies from the Hebrew Scriptures and declared them fulfilled (see Luke 4:16-21). He spoke with profound knowledge of the Jewish Scriptures, and people called Him "rabbi," a term for a Jewish religious teacher (see Matthew 26:25,49; Mark 9:5; 11:21; John 1:38; 3:2). Many of His sayings come directly from Jewish culture and customs.

Jesus' disciples and almost all of His earliest followers were Jewish, which reveals that believing in Jesus was a very "Jewish" thing to do. Although Jesus had disagreements with some of the religious leaders about how Judaism should be practiced, He never rejected the faith itself. Furthermore, there is no getting around the fact that the New Testament is a very Jewish book!

Given this, it is ironic that there has been such a thorny relationship between Jews and Christians in Western history. In truth, anti-Jewish attitudes are a perversion of the gospel and Scripture that must be renounced by followers of Jesus. Furthermore, if we want to understand the message of the book of Acts, we must learn to appreciate the Jewishness of the early Jesus movement. Many of the significant events of the New Testament that Luke depicts in Acts—including the Day of Pentecost—are tied to the rhythms of the Jewish religious calendar.

CHRIST, OUR PASSOVER

According to the Law of Moses, the Israelites were to assemble and appear before the Lord three times a year (see Exodus 23:14-19; 34:22-23; Deuteronomy 16:16). The first holy period was the Feast of Unleavened Bread (Passover). Held in early spring, it was a time to celebrate the Israelites' escape from slavery in Egypt (see Exodus 12–14).

In the original Passover in Egypt, the Hebrews did not have time to bake leavened bread—they had to make it without yeast. They killed a lamb, smeared its blood on the doorframe of their homes (so the death angel would "pass over" that house), and then cooked the lamb and ate it. The Jews recited these events every year at Passover. The New Testament poignantly calls Jesus "the Lamb of God, who takes away the sin of the world" (John 1:29) and "our Passover lamb" (1 Corinthians 5:7). At Jesus' last supper with His disciples, He linked His broken body and shed blood to the Passover (see Luke 22:19-20). Like the Hebrews in Egypt, by putting our trust in Jesus our Passover Lamb, we can escape spiritual death and inherit eternal life.

GOD'S GLORY, GOD'S SPIRIT, GOD'S PRESENCE

The second festival the Jews observed was the Feast of First Fruits, which celebrated the winter/spring harvest. It had two other names: (1) the Feast of Weeks, because it was held seven weeks after Passover; and (2) Pentecost, because it was held 50 days after Passover (*pente* in Greek means "50").

In Jewish tradition, the festival of First Fruits became associated with the Israelites' fearsome experience of encountering God at Mount Sinai (see session 1) and God's giving the Ten Commandments to Moses. During the feast, Exodus 19–20 and Ezekiel 1—in which the Word of the Lord came on Ezekiel through powerful, prophetic visions of God's glory— would be read out loud to the people.

Pentecost was a day of celebrating the awesome presence of God, God revealing Himself through His Spirit, the giving of God's Word to the people, fire from heaven, tremendous shaking, and other unexplainable supernatural events. Thus, in Acts 2:1-13, the worshipers in Jerusalem who came out of the Temple had just been meditating on the glory of the Lord. They had just heard about the majestic dwelling (or abiding or manifest) *presence* of God among His people at the high points during the Israelites' history (see Exodus 3:2-3; 13:21-22; 19–20; 24:9-10,16-17; 33:7-23; Leviticus 9:23-24; 2 Chronicles 7:1-3). The last time anything like these supernatural events had occurred was about 600 years before at the dedication of Solomon's Temple, when fire from heaven consumed the sacrifices and the glory of the Lord filled the Temple (see 2 Chronicles 7:1-3), but they knew that God had promised to do something amazing again (see Isaiah 40:3-5; 60:1-2,19; Ezekiel 44:4).

THE HOLY SPIRIT ARRIVES

Jesus' followers had previously witnessed God's glory by being with Christ (see Matthew 17:5; John 1:14; Acts 1:9). But on this day, the Day of Pentecost, God fulfilled the promises He had made to the Old Testament prophets *and* through Jesus—the "promise of the Father" (see Luke 24:49).

As the believers gather together in an upper room in Jerusalem as Jesus had instructed (see Acts 1:4), the glory of the Lord—God's presence in the Holy Spirit—comes full-force upon them. They hear a sound like the rushing of a mighty wind (recalling the violent shaking at Mount Sinai) and see tongues of fire (recalling fire from heaven) rest on each person. In this way, John the Baptist's prophecy that Jesus would baptize "with the Holy Spirit and fire" (Matthew 3:11; Luke 3:16) is fulfilled. The believers are filled with the Holy Spirit and are able to miraculously communicate what God has done in Christ to all the God-fearing Jews gathered in Jerusalem. This event represents the birth of the Church.

REVERSAL OF BABEL

In the story of the Tower of Babel told in Genesis 11:1-8, God confuses human languages and scatters the nations to the four corners of the earth. It could be argued that this was an act of mercy, an act of judgment, or both. Whatever it was, it is an acknowledgment that humanity is divided by tongues.

The Church's birthday is a reversal of this scene at the Tower of Babel. God-fearing Jews "from every nation under heaven" (Acts 2:5) and many scattered tongues come together in one place: Jerusalem. Divisions of culture and language are (at least temporarily) removed. This day gives the new Church a glimpse of what it can be: a place where God's Spirit dwells, exhibiting God's glory by breaking down racial, cultural and social barriers.

This picture is exactly what the apostle Paul had in mind when he wrote in Ephesians 2:11-22 about God breaking down walls of hostility between Jews and Gentiles and creating one new people in Christ. Paul perfectly captures one of the most central themes of Jesus' ministry: reconciling people to God and to each other. Similarly, in Galatians 3:26-29 he states that in Christ we are all God's children; no longer are we defined by whether we are Jews, Gentiles, men, women, slaves or free.

This perspective has a restorational point. In Genesis 1:26-27, God creates humanity in His image. In this original intention of God, all humans— of whatever race, culture, social status or gender—have innate nobility, dignity and worth. Sin, which is rebellion against God's intentions, ruins all of that and causes divisions, false stereotyping, feelings of superiority (and inferiority), deep suspicions, rivalries, fear, hatred and cruelty between individuals and groups of peoples. The gospel makes us realize that we're all in the same boat—we're sinful humans in need of healing and restoration from God. We forgive because we've been forgiven. We extend mercy because we've experienced mercy. We embrace because we've been embraced.

What's Going On?

When the God-fearing Jews who have gathered in Jerusalem from other nations hear the believers speaking in their own languages, they are bewildered and immediately want to know what is going on. Some make fun of them and say, "they have had too much wine" (Acts 2:13). So the apostle Peter stands up and begins to give an explanation to them in a way the Jewish crowd would understand.

THIS IS THAT

Peter's basic argument to the crowd is that *this* (what they see and hear before them now) is *that* (what was foretold by the prophets of old and by Jesus). In making this statement, he draws on several passages of Scripture from the Old Testament. The first passage comes from a "last days" prophecy of Joel (see Joel 2:28-32). In the Hebrew Scriptures, the "last days" refer to the time in the future when God fulfills His promises through the Messiah.

According to Joel's prophecy, two things will occur at this time: (1) God will pour out His Spirit on all peoples (not just the Jewish people); and (2) the prophetic Spirit of God will come upon sons and daughters (not discriminating based on gender), young and old (not discriminating on the basis of age), and upon men and women house-servants (not just the high-born or economically affluent).

This is exactly what happens in the rest of Acts. The arc of the book shows how the gospel progresses by God confirming the message of the gospel through miracles (see Acts 14:3), the willingness of the Church to be *marturioi* (martyr/witnesses) and suffer for the sake of Jesus, and God's providential leading and working behind the scenes. The Holy Spirit shows no favoritism; His power is not just for the apostles.

As the early Jesus movement rapidly grows, it continues the ministry of Jesus. Just as Jesus said, He would not leave His disciples orphaned but would come to them through the Holy Spirit (see John 14:18). Just as Jesus said, it was to the disciples' advantage that He go away (see John 16:7)—in other words, be crucified, resurrected and seated at God's right hand in the ascension—so that He and the Father could send the Holy Spirit (see John 14:26; 15:26), and so that the gifts of the Holy Spirit could be more liberally distributed (see 1 Corinthians 12:4-6). Just as in Jesus' earthly ministry, unusual leadings of God's Spirit, prophecy, signs and wonders (such as miracles of healing and freedom from unclean spirits) begin to take place. And just as when Jesus was on earth, God radically changes people from all levels of society and uses them to lead others to Him.

The prophecy Peter quotes from Joel also mentions things such as signs in the heavens and on earth, the sun being darkened and the moon turning to blood. This kind of language refers to the absolute end of time when God wraps everything up and brings history as we know it to a close.

THE GOSPEL PROCLAMATION

In Acts 2:22-24, we see how the earliest Church preached the gospel. Here Peter addresses the crowd as "fellow Israelites": they are not enemies, but they have a problem (sin and rebellion against God). Peter says that Jesus was a man approved by God, as evidenced by the miracles and wonders that accompanied His ministry. God's plan was for Jesus to go to the cross—but that Peter's fellow Israelites' sin was also responsible for putting Jesus to death. Peter goes on to add, "But God raised him from the dead, freeing him from the agony of death, because it was impossible for death to keep its hold on him" (verse 24). The cross and resurrection of Jesus the Messiah are the central message.

This presentation of the gospel is consistent throughout the rest of Acts (see 3:15; 4:2,33; 5:30; 13:33,38; 17:18; 18:28) as well as the rest of the New Testament (see Luke 24:46; Romans 4:25; 1 Corinthians 15:3; 2 Corinthians 5:15; Philippians 2:8; 1 Thessalonians 5:10; Hebrews 2:9; 1 Peter 3:18; Revelation 2:8). Jesus' death paid for our sins, but He is alive! Death couldn't hold Him. Therefore we can have hope not only in *this life* but also in the *life to come*. There is no better news than this!

The gospel message is not just about heaven, as great as that is. It is also a direct challenge to us to revise our values, follow God and address the human need we find on this earth. Among other things, through the Holy Spirit the Lord Jesus heals (see Acts 3:6; 9:34); gives courage and new life (see 4:13; 5:20); fulfills God's promises as Messiah (see 3:20; 5:42; 9:22); delivers the lost from the power of Satan (see 26:18); encourages martyrs at their point of death (see 8:55-56); baptizes with the Holy Spirit (see 1:5; 11:16); gives eternal life (see 13:48; 15:1); guides missionaries to where they should go (see 16:7); and advances the kingdom of God on earth (see 28:23,31).

DAVID'S SON; DAVID'S LORD

Peter continues his sermon in Acts 2:25-28 by quoting Psalm 16:8-11, a psalm attributed to David. In part, that quote reads, "You will not abandon me to the realm of the dead, you will not let your holy one see decay" (Acts 2:27).

Here it appears that David is saying, "I'm glad because You [God] will not abandon me [David] to the realm of the dead; You [God] will not allow me [David, God's "holy one"] to see the decay of death." But Peter points out to his listeners that David died—as they know, David's grave is present to this day. Therefore, the psalm must be talking about *somebody else* who is God's "holy one." Who might that be? Peter states that this holy one is Jesus, whom God raised from the dead, whose body saw no decay, and who is exalted, right now, at God's right hand (see Acts 2:29-34).

From the time they could speak, the Jewish people had said the *Shema Yisrael* every day: "Hear, O Israel, the LORD our God, the LORD is One" (Deuteronomy 6:4). Imagine the impact that Peter's statements would have had on them! He and the apostles were daring to modify the popular conception that Deuteronomy 6:4 meant God was *absolutely singular*. In Jesus, the apostles were now claiming that He is to be connected and identified with the Lord, who is still One, but not *absolutely singular*. Here we find an early expression of the deity of Jesus Christ, which in turn will lead to the understanding of the Trinity: that the One eternal God has eternally existed as God the Father, God the Son and God the Holy Spirit.

Peter follows up this theme with another of the early believers' favorite passages from the Hebrew Bible: Psalm 110. In this psalm, which is also attributed to David, "The LORD [God] says to my lord [David's Lord]: 'Sit at my [God's] right hand [place of authority] until I [God] make your [David's] enemies a footstool for your [David's] feet'" (verse 1). So, who was David's "Lord"?

Jesus Himself had used this psalm to make His claim of being God's unique Son (see Matthew 22:44; Mark 12:36; Luke 20:42). Together, Psalm 16:8-11 and Psalm 110 establish that the Messiah is "My Lord" and God's Son who, at the "right hand" of the Father, is in a divine position of authority. This terminology of Jesus being at the right hand of God is a central affirmation throughout the New Testament (see Matthew 26:64; Mark 14:62; 16:19; Luke 22:65; Acts 5:31; 7:55-56; Romans 8:34; Ephesians 1:20; Colossians 3:1; Hebrews 1:3,13; 8:1; 10:12; 12:2; 1 Peter 3:22; Revelation 1:16,17,20; 2:1; 5:1).

The Final Ingathering

Returning to the discussion of the Jewish community's three major feasts, the third was the Feast of Ingathering, which was a celebration of the fall harvest. It was also called the Feast of Trumpets. The Day of Atonement followed this feast 10 days later (see Leviticus 23:23-28; Numbers 29:1-10).

In Jewish tradition, at this festival the priests presented two loaves to God. Unlike the Feast of Unleavened Bread, these loaves symbolized the end of the harvest and were to have leaven in them. The two leavened loaves in the Feast of Ingathering represented the Jewish people and those who would come to believe in God from among the non-Jewish people.

Given this understanding, we are awaiting that glorious day when God blows the trumpet for the end of time and gathers His people from among the Jews and Gentiles—one people in Christ. Until then, as best we can, and with the help of the Holy Spirit, we follow Jesus' life and proclaim the gospel to all. We sow the seeds, believing that God's Holy Spirit brings the harvest, opens hearts and draws people to Himself.

QUESTIONS FOR PERSONAL APPLICATION AND DISCUSSION

How does the information in this session about the Jewish background of Acts help you to better understand the book?

_____

_____

_____

What is the link between the Passover lamb in the Old Testament and Jesus in the New Testament? What is the link between the Feast of First Fruits in the Old Testament and the Day of Pentecost in the book of Acts?

_____

_____

_____

What did the Jews celebrate on Pentecost? What did the believers and the disciples experience in the upper room? What did God fulfill on this day?

_____

_____

_____

How does the infilling of the Holy Spirit on Pentecost represent a reversal of the scene of the Tower of Babel in Genesis 11:1-8?

_____

_____

_____

_____

When God-fearing Jews who had gathered in Jerusalem from various nations heard the believers speaking in their own languages, they wanted an explanation of what was going on. What was one theory put forth by people in the crowd? How did Peter respond to this comment in Acts 2:14-15?

_____

_____

_____

_____

What was Peter's basic argument of what was occurring? What support does he use to make his statements?

_____

_____

_____

_____

What was Peter's basic proclamation of the gospel message? What hope did he give the God-fearing Jews who had assembled to listen to him?

_____

_____

_____

_____

In Acts 2:25-30, Peter quotes Psalm 16:8-11 (attributed to King David) and states that because David is dead, the psalm must be speaking of *somebody else* who is God's "holy one." Why would this have been controversial to Peter's primarily Jewish audience?

_____

_____

_____

_____

How do Psalm 16:8-11 and Psalm 110 both establish that Jesus is God's unique Son?

_____

_____

_____

_____

_____

What is the connection between the Feast of Ingathering in the Old Testament and the events of Jesus' Second Coming in the New Testament?

_____

_____

_____

_____

_____

Sources

Henrietta C. Mears, *What the Bible Is All About,* "Understanding Acts" (Ventura, CA: Regal Books, 2011), chapter 31.

Mears, *Highlights of Scripture, Part Four: Words and Works of Jesus, Teacher's Book* (Los Angeles, CA: The Gospel Light Press, 1937).

THOSE AWESOME JESUS WOMEN

Partners in the Gospel (Luke–Acts)

SESSION FOCUS

The status and role of women in the early Jesus movement.

KEY VERSE TO MEMORIZE

*There is neither Jew nor Gentile, neither slave nor free, nor is there
male and female, for you are all one in Christ Jesus.*
GALATIANS 3:28

WEEKLY READING

DAY 1	Proverbs 31
DAY 2	Luke 1
DAY 3	Psalms 2; 9; 10; 34; 73
DAY 4	Luke 7:36-50; John 4
DAY 5	Romans 16:1-16; 1 Corinthians 14:26-40; 1 Timothy 2

FOR LEADERS: SESSION AT A GLANCE

SESSION OUTLINE	60 MIN.	90 MIN.	WHAT YOU WILL DO
Getting started	10	15	Pray and worship
Main points of the chapter	25	35	Discuss how Jesus is God's Word to us
Application and discussion	15	25	Discuss the role of women in Luke and Acts and in our own Jesus movements today
Looking ahead	5	5	Prepare for next week
Wrapping up	5	10	Close with prayer or song

The Status of Women in Ancient Societies

Sometimes, you will hear sentiments from people like this: "Organized religions are sexist . . . all of them are as simple as that." Whatever people might mean by "organized," with regard to the early Jesus movement, the role of women definitely wasn't "as simple as that." Women were extremely important in the Jesus movement, as seen especially in the Gospel of Luke and Acts. This high valuation of women was markedly different from the situation most women faced in the Greco-Roman culture of the time.

KEEPING WOMEN IN THEIR PLACE

On the whole, Greco-Roman society during the first century was intensely male-dominated, patriarchal and oppressive to women. Men enjoyed power and influence, and slaves were considered property. Women were a little higher in position than slaves, but they were still considered the property of the male head of the household.

Some of the writers of the time capture this view toward women. The Greek philosopher Xenophon (c. 430–354 BC) wrote, "God from the first adapted the woman's nature, I think, to the indoor and man's to the outdoor tasks . . . [and] meted out a larger share of fear to the woman than to the man."[1] Aristotle (384–322 BC) quipped, "Let it be [a woman's] aim to obey her husband; giving no heed to public affairs, nor having any part in arranging the marriages of her children. Rather, when the time shall come to give or receive in marriage sons or daughters, let her then hearken to her husband in all respects, and agreeing with him obey his wishes."[2] Lucius Valerius Flaccus (d. 180 BC), a Roman consul, put it even more succinctly: "Never, while her men are well, is a woman's slavery cast off."[3]

There was a massive double standard in Greco-Roman society in terms of morals. Unmarried women were expected to be chaste, and married women were supposed to have children, keep the home fires burning, make meals and watch over the extended household (children, slaves and extended family members). Single men, on the other hand, weren't expected to be chaste, and married men weren't expected to be faithful to their wives. Men were free to carouse around, have mistresses and concubines, and to go to the temples to "worship" with temple prostitutes.

Marriages were arranged. Daughters had little or no say in whom they married—they had to marry whomever their parents chose for them. If something went wrong and a marriage dissolved, the divorced woman could be left destitute. Divorce was assumed to be the woman's fault.

JUDAISM, A MUCH BETTER DEAL

Women in Jewish culture fared much better. Wives were honored as partners in marriage and as noble women whose worth was "far more than rubies" (Proverbs 31:10). They were not considered chattel property as they were in the surrounding culture, and the ideal for marriage was one man and one woman. Divorce was permitted but socially disapproved. Because faithfulness in marriage was so highly prized, Jewish men were not to have mistresses or concubines or visit pagan temple prostitutes, and Jewish women were forbidden from being prostitutes in pagan temples. Women were also extolled to dress and act modestly.

Education was valued. Women were expected to know the Torah well enough to teach their children up to a certain age, so they were taught to read and write. Wives were responsible for taking care of the ritual aspects in the home: to light the Sabbath candle, to tithe and to follow the rules of kosher food. Women were the sanctifiers of the home, just as the priests were the sanctifiers of the Temple (see 2 Chronicles 29:5).

Marriages were arranged, but daughters could refuse the proposed husband. If a woman was widowed, she could not be thrown out of her home. If she was divorced, a payment had to be made to her.

Women could possess property and were encouraged to take part in their own businesses (see Proverbs 31). Some became philosophers and teachers (see Acts 18:26). Some rose to leadership, just like famous women in the Hebrew Bible such as Miriam, Moses' sister; Deborah, a prophetess, judge and "mother" of Israel; Huldah, a prophetess and advisor to King Josiah; and Esther, a queen of Persia, who wound up saving her people.

Yes, Jewish society was still patriarchal. But in contrast to the surrounding cultures, Jewish women had a much better deal.

Luke's Perspective on Women in His Gospel

Luke was deeply influenced by Jesus' and Paul's attitudes and actions toward women. Both Jesus and Paul elevated women well beyond the better deal that women had in Jewish society.

Jesus, Paul and Luke were sharply attuned to the Bible's teaching on human dignity—a teaching that goes all the way back to creation. In Genesis 1:26-27, God creates men and women in His own image and likeness. Note that both males *and* females are created in God's image—women are not inferior! In Genesis 2:18, God scoops out Adam's side and creates an equal partner for him. These passages sketch out God's original intention, which has sadly often been trampled underfoot or ignored.

This principle of human dignity based on being created in the image of God extends to all people of every culture and ethnic group—men and women, rich and poor, high and low, well connected in society and marginalized. Luke picked up on this principle and prominently features women in his Gospel and in Acts. We will mention only a few of the women he includes in his writings here.

MARY, THE MOTHER OF JESUS

In Luke 1, the angel Gabriel announces that Mary will give birth to the Messiah, and Elizabeth gives her a word of prophecy that she is blessed among women (see verse 42). When Mary hears this, she launches into a song that we know as the "Magnificat." Her faith comes through clear and strong in these verses. Mary sings about God's mercy and faithfulness through the generations, and then she expresses one of Luke's key themes: the Great Reversal. The high and mighty will be brought low, and the lowly will be lifted up. The rich will be sent away, and the hungry will be filled.

From where did Mary get this theme? She got it from a profound understanding of the story of the Exodus, when God freed the Israelites (the poor) in Egypt from Pharaoh (the mighty). Her song shrewdly summarizes psalms such as Psalm 2, in which the Messiah puts down the (mighty) nations' rebellion against God's kingdom; Psalms 9 and 10, which speak of God's justice; and Psalms 34 and 73, which speak of God righting wrongs. Her song also distills the message of Israel's prophets, which follow along similar lines as the psalms.

Jesus preached this same theme in His blessed-are-the-poor sermon, which also has a woe-to-the-rich element (see Luke 6:20-26). This theme continues in parables such as Lazarus and the Rich Man (see Luke 16:19-31) and the Camel and a Needle's Eye (see Matthew 19:23-30).[4] Luke's Gospel puts a new twist on the Great Reversal theme, applying it to those who thought they were "in" and "okay" simply because they happened to be born Jewish. Jesus says that if they have no faith, the Gentiles, who previously were far from God and His promises, will replace them (see Luke 3:8; 13:28).

A FEW GOOD WOMEN

Jesus had a group of loyal women followers, some of whom Luke mentions by name. One of these was Mary Magdalene, a woman who is somewhat enigmatic in Christian tradition.[5] According to the New Testament, Mary Magdalene was a prominent and important disciple. She is mentioned in Luke 8:1-3, along with some other women who "had been cured of evil spirits and diseases."

Mary Magdalene stood by Jesus at the cross (see Matthew 27:55-56; Mark 15:40), kept watch at Jesus' tomb and brought spices to anoint Jesus' body (see Matthew 27:61; 28:1; Mark 15:47; 16:1; Luke 24:1,10; John 20:1,11,18). Jesus appeared to His women followers first, and Mary Magdalene was among them (see Luke 24:10). An angel told the women to go quickly and tell the other apostles what they had seen (see Matthew 28:5-7), and when they did, the men dismissed their tale, thinking what they said was the nonsense of weak-minded women (see Luke 24:11). The men's response revealed their lack of faith and quite possibly some latent prejudice against women.

As we have seen, the word "apostles" means those who are appointed and sent. The angel appointed and sent Mary Magdalene and the other women to notify the disciples, making these women "apostles to the apostles." Unfortunately, later Christian tradition was afflicted by male bias and prejudice against women. In AD 591, Pope Gregory wrote a homily on Luke's Gospel in which he stated, "She whom Luke calls the sinful woman, whom John calls Mary, we believe to be the Mary from whom seven devils were ejected according to Mark."[6] By associating Mary Magdalene with the unnamed sinful woman of Luke 7:36-50 (and then with other sinful, adultress women), Mary Magdalene—the faithful disciple who was among the first witnesses to the resurrection of Christ—was turned into "the repentant whore."

Another of the women Luke names in Acts 8:1-3 is Joanna, the wife of Chuza. Joanna's husband managed Herod's household affairs. This reference to Joanna shows that the early Jesus movement not only reached the common people but also into the highest levels of society. Joanna also kept vigil at the cross (see Luke 24:1).

We don't know anything about Susanna, who is mentioned in this one place alone. Luke tells us that "many" others supported Jesus' ministry from their own financial resources. This shows that the early Jesus movement was a cooperative effort of men and women working together, and that to some extent it was *dependent* on women's contributions.

A FEW BAD WOMEN

Jesus reached out to everyone, including people of low reputation. He ate with tax collectors and sinners (see Matthew 9:10-13; 11:19; Mark 2:15-17;

Luke 5:27-32; 15:2). He showed great respect to the sinful woman who anointed His feet with tears (see Luke 7:36-50). He took time to speak with the Samaritan woman at the well, even though she had been married five times and was currently living with a man who was not her husband (see John 4). Jesus didn't hold peoples' past sins against them but always gave them opportunity for self-reflection and the chance to get a new start on life.

Luke's Perspective on Women in Acts

In the book of Acts, Luke continues to illustrate the importance of women leaders alongside the men in the early Christian movement. He counts women (specifically naming Mary, the mother of Jesus) among the post-resurrection band of Messianic believers who had joined together and were constantly in prayer, waiting for Jesus' promise of the Holy Spirit (see Acts 1:14). The women were there with the men when the Holy Spirit came upon them all on the Day of Pentecost (see 2:1). It wasn't just the men who were baptized in the Holy Spirit; the women were full partakers as well (see Acts 2:17-18; 21:8-9; 1 Corinthians 12:4-11). As the early Jesus movement grew, women were integral to the early fellowship of believers (see Acts 2:42-47; 4:32-39; 17:4,12,34).

WOMEN AS DEACONS

In Acts 6, Luke introduces us to the role of deacons (Greek *diakonos*) and their service in the Jesus movement. In Acts 6:1-4, the Twelve gather all of the disciples together and appoint seven men "full of the Spirit and wisdom" to meet both physical and spiritual needs in the Church. Two of these men included Stephen, who became the Church's first martyr, and Philip, who took care of widows' needs but was by no means limited only to that kind of service (see 6:5). In Acts 8, he evangelized (see verse 5), performed healings and cast out demons (see verses 6-7), followed prophetic guidance (see verse 26), taught the Scriptures (see verses 31-35), and baptized (see verses 36-37).

Significantly, in Romans 16 Paul provides evidence of his reliance on women fellow co-workers in bringing the gospel to the Gentiles. He calls one woman named Phoebe a "deacon" in the church at Cencheraea (see 16:1). Like Brother Philip, Sister Phoebe was also a deacon. Paul enjoined the church in Rome to receive her worthily and to give her any help she needed, because she had been a benefactor to many, including himself (see 16:2).

WOMEN AS GATEKEEPERS

The early Jesus movement was a house church movement. As a persecuted minority, the fledgling Church didn't have the time or the resources to build worship structures for the community. The believers needed to operate under the radar of the authorities. In these house churches, women sometimes served as gatekeepers—shepherds who protected their flocks from false teachers. The businesswoman Lydia helped found one of the strongest churches in the New Testament at Philippi (see Acts 16:13-15). Paul greeted "Nympha and the church in her house" (Colossians 4:15). In 2 John 1:1-5, John "the elder" addresses his letter to another female gatekeeper, referring to her as "the chosen lady" and "dear lady."

WOMEN AS MEMBERS OF PAUL'S APOSTOLIC BAND

In Acts 18, we discover two more fellow-workers with Paul: Aquila and Priscilla. The first time Luke mentions this couple, he places Aquila's name first (see verse 2). At the time, it was customary when presenting names to mention the more prestigious name first. For married couples in a patriarchal society, first place would normally go to the man. But in Acts 18:18,26 and Romans 16:4, that order is reversed. Paul breaks with tradition and names Priscilla first, because she is the one taking the lead in upfront leadership. In Romans 16:3, Paul even calls her "Prisca," a shortened, familiar way of saying Priscilla. Paul commends Prisca and Aquila as "my fellow workers in Christ" who risked their lives for him.

Paul named at least one woman apostle. In Romans 16:7, he states that Andronicus and Junia—who were either a married couple or brother and sister—were "outstanding among the apostles." The two might have been blood relatives of Paul, but were more likely fellow Jewish believers and countrymen (the Greek word *sungenes* can refer to both). Here again, Paul bucks the male-only leadership model, awarding Junia the title of apostle.[7]

WOMEN AS PROPHETS

We have already observed how Peter quoted Joel's prophecy of an outpouring of the Spirit on men and women of all classes and said that it had begun to be fulfilled. Acts 21:8-9 tells us that Philip (the same Philip of Acts 6 and 8) had four unmarried daughters who prophesied. Also, Paul assumes that women will prophesy in church (see 1 Corinthians 11:5; 14:26-33) and even encourages that to happen (see 1 Corinthians 12:31; 14:1). Women were active in the early churches, and Paul's practice and letters show conclusively that he considered this a good thing. Paul even went out of his way to elevate women: "There is neither Jew nor Gentile, neither slave nor free, nor is there male and female, for you are all one in Christ Jesus" (Galatians 3:28).

Paul's statements in 1 Corinthians 14:34-35 have caused controversy in some churches because, taken in isolation, they seem to be restrictive and even repressive statements about what roles women can have in church. However, since we now see Paul's actual practice, we can say with confidence that these verses cannot refer to an absolute ban on women speaking publicly at church gatherings or a prohibition on women having positions of leadership. More likely, Paul was either quoting a Corinthian slogan or quotation, or he was addressing a specific practice in the Corinthian church that needed to be corrected.

Likewise, Paul's words in 1 Timothy 2:11-15 have raised controversy about the roles that women should be allowed to perform in church. But again, this instruction seems to be directed at a particular setting. Many scholars believe that some women in the church in Ephesus—most likely younger widows—were involved in promoting a false teaching (see 1 Timothy 5:11-15). Paul was attempting to prohibit them from deceiving others. Given the context, there is no real indication here that Paul is addressing women in general in these remarks.

WOMEN AS MARTYRS

In Acts 6:8–7:60, Luke relates the story of Stephen, the first martyr of the early Jesus movment. It is a moving tale. Following hard on Stephen's death, a brutal, terrorizing foe came against the church in the form of Saul of Tarsus. Saul was a zealous Pharisee. He waged a merciless campaign against the believers in Jesus, dragging many unnamed women and men into prison and to their deaths (see Acts 8:3; 9:2; 22:4; 26:10).

Jesus had said that those who decided to follow Him might experience humiliating death (see Luke 9:23-24). He had told His disciples, "I tell you, whoever publicly acknowledges me before others, the Son of Man will also acknowledge before the angels of God. But whoever disowns me before others will be disowned before the angels of God" (Luke 12:8-9). He had also told His followers, "You will be betrayed even by parents, brothers and sisters, relatives and friends, and they will put some of you to death. Everyone will hate you because of me. But not a hair of your head will perish. Stand firm, and you will win life" (Luke 21:16-19).

These sisters of the "fairer sex" might have avoided persecution and martyrdom by keeping silent, but they didn't. They courageously confessed their faith in Jesus and did not shrink back from death. In history, they have been followed by thousands of other noble examples.

QUESTIONS FOR PERSONAL APPLICATION AND DISCUSSION

What were some of the attitudes toward women in Greco-Roman culture? What were women not allowed to do? How did attitudes in Jewish culture differ?

_____

_____

_____

_____

What was Luke's perspective on women? What was Paul's perspective?

_____

_____

_____

_____

What was Jesus' perspective on women? What is meant by the term "the Great Reversal"?

_____

_____

_____

_____

_____

One of the women who figures prominently in Scripture is Mary, the mother of Jesus. Her song in Luke 1:46-55 (the Magnificat) is a remarkable testament to her profound faith in the God of the Hebrew Scriptures. What did she express in this song? What did she see God doing through Christ?

_____

_____

_____

_____

Another woman who figures prominently in the Gospels is Mary Magdalene, who appears to have been an important disciple in the early Jesus movement. With whom was Mary identified in later Christian tradition? What was the motive behind this? How did this serve to diminish her role?

_____

_____

_____

_____

_____

Not all of the women mentioned in the Bible were followers of Christ. Herodias (c. 15 BC–AD 39) was first married to Herod II, her half-uncle, but then divorced him to marry Herod Antipas (the Herod before whom Jesus appeared). John the Baptist criticized Herod Antipas for this marriage, which led to John being arrested. Read Mark 6:17-29. What role did Herodias and her daughter, Salome, play in John's death?

_____

_____

_____

_____

_____

What does this indicate about her status?

_____

_____

_____

_____

Based on Paul's writings, we see that women were active in early churches and that many held important roles. Given this, why have Paul's statements in 1 Corinthians 14:34-35 and 1 Timothy 2:11-15 caused controversy? Is Paul making a general statement about women in these verses? Why or why not?

_____

_____

_____

_____

_____

What attitudes toward women have you seen in today's Church? Do you think these attitudes are justified according to Scripture? Why or why not?

_____

_____

_____

_____

_____

Stephen was the first Christian martyr, but many more followed—including women. What had Jesus told His disciples about the cost of following Him? What promise does He offer in John 16:33 to those who remain faithful to Him even at the point of death?

_____

_____

_____

_____

_____

How would His words have inspired those in the Jesus movement?

_____

_____

_____

_____

_____

Notes

1. Xenophon, "On Men and Women," cited in William Stearns Davis, ed., *Readings in Ancient History: Illustrative Extracts from the Sources* (Boston, MA: Allyn and Bacon, 1912-1913), vol. 1, pp. 265-271.
2. Aristotle, "On a Good Wife," cited in Edward English Walford and John Gillies, trans., *The Politics and Economics of Aristotle* (London: G. Bell & Sons, 1908).
3. Lucius Valerius Flaccus, cited in Livy, "Women Demonstrate and Obtain Repeal of the Oppian Law," *The History of Rome,* vol. 34, no. 1.
4. For an extended discussion of Jesus' parables, see sessions 7–12 in *The Life of Jesus* (Ventura, CA: Gospel Light, 2011) in the *What the Bible Is All About* Bible Study Series.
5. Traditionally, the name "Magdalene" has been interpreted to mean that this Mary was from Magdala, a town on the western shore of the Sea of Galilee (Luke says she was actually called "Magdalene"). While opinions vary, there are believed to be at least six Marys in the New Testament: (1) Mary, the mother of Jesus (see Luke 3:23); (2) Mary Magdalene; (3) Mary of Bethany, the sister of Martha and Lazarus (see Luke 10:38-42); (4) Mary, the mother of Mark and sister of Barnabas

(see Acts 12:12; Colossians 4:10); (5) Mary, the mother of James and Joses (see Mark 15:40), also believed to be the wife of Clopas (see John 19:25) and "the other Mary" mentioned in Matthew 27:61; and (6) Mary of Rome (see Romans 16:6).

6. Pope Gregory the Great, Homily 33, cited in Susan Haskins, *Mary Magdalene: The Essential History* (New York: Pimlico, 2003), p. 96.

7. Some scholars have claimed that Junia couldn't have been a woman because Paul would never have named a woman to leadership over men, and that in the Greek text of Romans 16:7 the name Iounian (the accusative form) is an abbreviation for the male name Iounianus ("Junianus"). However, there is no evidence that the masculine name Iounianus existed in the Roman Empire. Dr. Peter Lampe, Professor of New Testament at Union Theological Seminary in Richmond, Virginia, says, "Without exception the Church Fathers in late antiquity identified Andronicus' partner in Romans 16:7 as a woman, as did minuscule 33 in the 9th century which records iounia with an acute accent [indicating a female personal name]. Only later medieval copyists of Romans 16:7 could not imagine a woman being an apostle and wrote the masculine name 'Junias.' This latter name did not exist in antiquity; its explanation as a Greek abbreviation of the Latin name 'Junianus' is unlikely" (Dr. Peter Lampe, "Junias," Anchor Bible Dictionary [New York: Doubleday, 1992], vol. 3, p. 1127).

Sources

Henrietta C. Mears, *What the Bible Is All About,* "Understanding Acts" (Ventura, CA: Regal Books, 2011), chapter 31.

Mears, *Highlights of Scripture, Part Four: Words and Works of Jesus, Teacher's Book* (Los Angeles, CA: The Gospel Light Press, 1937).

MARKS OF THE MOVEMENT
A Supernatural Fellowship (Acts 3–5:11)

SESSION FOCUS

The unique characteristics of the early Jesus movement and how its members endured in the face of persecution.

KEY VERSES TO MEMORIZE

With great power the apostles continued to testify to the resurrection of the Lord Jesus. And God's grace was so powerfully at work in them all that there were no needy persons among them.
ACTS 4:33-34

WEEKLY READING

DAY 1	Acts 3
DAY 2	Acts 4
DAY 3	Psalm 2
DAY 4	Acts 5:1-11
DAY 5	Joshua 7

FOR LEADERS: SESSION AT A GLANCE

SESSION OUTLINE	60 MIN.	90 MIN.	WHAT YOU WILL DO
Getting started	10	15	Pray and worship
Main points of the chapter	25	35	Discuss how Jesus is God's Word to us
Application and discussion	15	25	Discuss the distinct new life exhibited by the followers of Jesus and the implications their example has for us
Looking ahead	5	5	Prepare for next week
Wrapping up	5	10	Close with prayer or song

Defining the Jesus Movement

Acts is the infancy narrative of the Church. In Acts 1, Jesus promised the disciples that He would send the Holy Spirit, and in Acts 2 the promised Holy Spirit arrived. The remainder of the book will answer the question, "Now what?"

The Jesus believers had a fresh slate. There was no set path for them to follow. They had to work through things as they went along, relying on what they knew about God from the Hebrew Bible (the Old Testament), on what they remembered from their personal experiences with Jesus, and also on the intimate presence of the Holy Spirit. It was a time of Spirit-enabling experimentation. Those in the Early Church had to do a lot of creative trailblazing.

THEN AND NOW

In our modern times, we have 2,000 years of Christian tradition and history to look back on to help guide our actions. But in Acts, "Christianity" didn't yet exist. When we hear the word "church," we immediately start thinking about buildings. But in Acts, the church was wherever you could find followers of Jesus. Today, Christian meetings are relatively respected social events, but in Acts, respecting social conventions was not high on the agenda. For these reasons, it is perilous to try to push the earliest Jesus movement into whatever molds we have created for our idea of "church."

It is also important not to read too much from our own experience when we see the phrase "word of God" in Acts. In our minds, the term refers to the whole Bible—including the Old and New Testaments—but we have to remember that the New Testament did not yet exist. In the early Jesus movement, the ministry of God's word is always tied to the power of the Holy Spirit—the two go hand in hand. For the apostles, this includes preaching the gospel, teaching a new understanding of the Hebrew Bible (showing how the prophecies all point toward Christ), and cooperating with (or at least not hindering) the surprising new supernatural things the Holy Spirit is doing.

NAMING THE JESUS MOVEMENT

So far, we've been referring to the believers in Acts as members of the early "Jesus movement." This is because up to this point, the movement didn't actually have an established name. What did the earliest believers in Jesus call themselves? And what did others call them?

First and foremost, it's important to note that almost all of the early believers considered themselves to be Jews. They didn't consider themselves "the New Testament Church," because the New Testament had not yet been written. They didn't consider themselves "Jewish Christians" or "Hebrew Christians," because the name "Christian" hadn't yet been invented (see Acts 11:26).

While some of Jesus' first followers had not been born Jewish, they had attached themselves to Judaism as God-fearers, proselytes and converts. *God-fearers* could go to Jewish synagogue meetings for worship and contribute to the community through the synagogue, but they weren't recognized as Jews. *Proselytes* were people on the path toward officially changing their religion and becoming Jewish. *Converts* were those who had completed all the requirements of Judaism and had been accepted as members into the Jewish community.

From Acts 2:47 forward, Luke begins to use the Greek word *ekklesia* ("to summon forth" or "to call out from") to describe the early Jesus movement. The word itself, which is typically translated as "church," does not refer to a building or even a formal structure but merely implies that a group is assembling. For example, in Acts 2:47, we know from the context that when Luke states, "The Lord added to the church [*ekklesia*] daily such as should be saved" (*KJV*), he is referring to those in the early Jesus movement. In Acts 19:32, however, he uses the same word when referring to a gathering of townspeople from Ephesus—some of which included idol makers: "The assembly [*ekklesia*] was in confusion."

Another early name that Luke uses for the movement is "the Way" (see Acts 9:2; 19:9,23; 22:4; 24:14,22). The people who followed the Way were first called "Christians" in Syrian Antioch, which is in present-day Antakya, Turkey (see Acts 11:26). In Acts 20:28, the Church is also called a "flock," repeating a metaphor that Jesus had used (see Luke 12:32). The Jews who did not believe in Jesus considered the Jesus movement a sect within Judaism (see Acts 24:5; 28:22), much like the sects of the Sadducees (see Acts 5:17) and the Pharisees (see Acts 15:5; 26:5). Some of the Jews considered it a harmless sect, while others wanted to stamp it out.

ROMAN PERSECUTION OF CHRISTIANS

The Romans prided themselves on their religious tolerance. However, over time they began to get suspicious of the Christians because of their secret meetings (were the Christians planning sedition?) and troubling rumors of cannibalism (why were the Christians "eating flesh" in their rituals?). They considered the Christians atheists (why wouldn't they acknowledge Caesar as divine?) and blasphemers (why wouldn't they sacrifice to the Romans' gods?).

Early Roman historians tended to dismiss Christians as a troubling sect of Judaism or as a superstitious cult. Tacitus (AD 56–117), the first historian to mention a person named "Christus," states that He "suffered the extreme penalty during the reign of Tiberius at the hands of one of our procurators, Pontius Pilatus, and a most mischievous superstition, thus checked for the moment, again broke out not only in Judea, the first source of the evil, but even in Rome."[1] Suetonius (AD 69/75–130), another Roman historian, writes that during the reign of Emperor Claudius, "The Jews constantly made disturbances at the instigation of Chrestus . . . [so he] expelled them from Rome."[2] Suetonius adds that later, during the reign of Emperor Nero, "Punishment was inflicted on the Christians, a class of men given to a new and mischievous superstition."[3]

This imperially sanctioned persecution of Christians came in AD 64, shortly after a great fire broke out in Rome that virtually obliterated the city. While it is uncertain as to who or what started the fire, many Romans blamed the Emperor Nero, who wanted to build a grand palatial complex in the heart of the city. Nero needed a scapegoat, and in this he found Christians to be an easy target. As Tacitus reports, "To get rid of the report, Nero fastened the guilt and inflicted the most exquisite tortures on a class hated for their abominations, called Chrestians by the populace."[4]

Nero ordered Christians to be thrown to dogs and other wild beasts, crucified and burned to serve as lights for the city. According to Christian tradition, it was under his rule that Peter and Paul were put to death as leaders of this "dangerous" movement. By portraying Christian faith as a "foreign superstition," Nero was able to gain support for the need to suppress this new religious sect with the cruelest force.

Marks of the Movement

In previous sessions, we have discussed how the early Jesus movement was centered on the risen Christ. The Jesus people believed that He was the Jewish Messiah promised by God in the Hebrew Scriptures. Jesus was not just for the Jews but was the Savior for all the peoples of the world. The Jesus people were full of astonishment and joy at God's power and good-

ness in raising Christ from the dead (see Luke 24:41). They were benefici-
aries of the Holy Spirit and saw the continuation of Jesus' ministry in the
gifts of the Spirit (see Acts 1–2). They modified their cultural training and
became more inclusive of women and Gentiles (a story that will gradually
unfold). Yet there was even more that distinguished this new movement.

A FELLOWSHIP OF TEACHING, PRAYER AND HEALING

In Acts 2:42-47 and 4:32-35, Luke gives us an intimate portrait of what the
Church was like in those first few days. It was a teaching-fest (and love-
fest) that went on for some time (we don't know how long). During this extended conference-like setting, the new believers got a whole new look at
the Scriptures (see Luke 24:44).

The believers also prayed together, got to know one another, and "broke
bread" together—a term that can refer to regular meals or to reenacting the
Last Supper, as Jesus had taught His apostles to do. They witnessed miracles of healing. They shared what they had with each another. Some sold
real estate to fund this amazing birthing moment. They met in homes.
God's grace was on them. And each day, the Lord brought more and more
people into the fellowship. It must have been an incredibly exciting time!

A CROSS-CULTURAL FELLOWSHIP

In Acts 2, Luke mentions how Jews descended on Jerusalem from all corners of the Mediterranean. In the coming years, this wide scattering and re-
gathering of Jews from many cultural basins would be mirrored in the
Church as the gospel radiated outward from Jerusalem to Judea to Samaria
and finally to non-Jews in the farthest corners of the earth (see Acts 1:8). As
it traveled, it broke down ethnic barriers and reached out across cultural
lines. From this we see that from its earliest days, Christianity was a God-
serving, people-loving, cross-cultural missionary movement.

A NEW ATTITUDE TOWARD WEALTH

Our modern consumer culture constantly preaches that the more we have,
the more we spend and the more we acquire, the more valuable we are as
human beings, the happier we are, and the more superior we are in the
grand scheme of things.

Gospel values are quite different. The gospel says that everything we
have—our time, health, talents and treasure—is a gift from God. Therefore,
we are to take the resources God gives us and use them to God's glory. Jesus

wants us to serve others and give ourselves away. This is exactly what we see happening in the early fellowship.

In one scene told in Acts 3:1-10, Peter and John come across a lame beggar and heal him in the name of Jesus. Notice what they say to the beggar right before they heal him: "Silver or gold I do not have, but what I do have I give you. In the name of Jesus Christ of Nazareth, walk" (verse 6). Peter and John weren't prancing along in smooth clothes and fancy suits, showing off their bling or constantly making big pitches for money. Getting rich off their followers was the furthest thing from their minds.

Healings, Confessions and Wonders

In Acts 3:11-26, Luke presents Peter's second sermon to onlookers (the first took place on the Day of Pentecost in Acts 2:14-41). On this occasion, the crowd had just witnessed the disciples heal a lame man, and they were astonished and wanted to know what was going on. In response, Peter addresses the crowd by directly appealing to their conscience. His objective is to tell the truth in love and point them to God's longing to forgive sinners and bring them into fellowship with Himself.

Peter begins by presenting God's view of history. He states that everything in the Law and the Prophets (the Old Testament) has led up to this present moment. Two thousand years earlier, God had made an ironclad promise to Abraham that through Abraham's descendant (Christ!), all the families of the peoples on earth would be blessed (see Genesis 18:18). Peter then defines what "blessing" means—it's not just a pat on the head. Rather, God had raised Jesus from the dead to bless them by turning them from their wickedness, their cruelty and their foolishness (see Acts 3:26). God's promises have now come full circle. He is a promise-keeping God.

FEARLESS CONFESSION

The events Luke depicts in Acts 3 take place in the Jerusalem Temple precincts in an area known as "Solomon's Porch" or "Solomon's Colonnade" (see also John 10:23; Acts 5:12). The colonnade was located on the eastern side of the Temple and had many stone columns capped by a roof enclosure to provide shade. In Acts 4:1-21, the Temple guards seize Peter and John from this location and haul them before the Sanhedrin (the Jewish ruling council). The council asks the disciples by whose power they are doing these miracles, to which Peter replies, "It is by the name of Jesus

Christ of Nazareth, whom you crucified but whom God raised from the dead" (verse 10). The council demands that Peter and John stop preaching about the resurrection of Jesus, but they answer boldly and with great conviction. For the time being the council lets them go, because they cannot deny that a significant miracle has taken place.

PRAYER, SIGNS AND WONDERS

After Peter and John are released from the council, they relate what happened to "their own people" (the church). The response? One of the most amazing prayers in the Bible (see Acts 4:23-31).

As previously noted, the members of the early Jesus movement understood that all the Scripture shed light on Jesus and His mission. So they consider the events that have occurred to Peter and John and interpret them prophetically in light of Psalm 2, a highly significant and major text for understanding the Hebrew Bible. They pray, "Sovereign Lord . . . You spoke by the Holy Spirit through the mouth of your servant, our father David: 'Why do the nations rage and the peoples plot in vain? The kings of the earth rise up and the rulers band together against the Lord and against his anointed one'" (Acts 4:25-26; see also Psalm 2:1-2). For the early believers, this passage predicted that human rulers would oppose the "anointed one" (the Lord's Messiah), but that God would overcome this opposition.

While Luke does not record everything for which the church prayed on this occasion, it is important to note that he does not record the believers praying for the persecution to cease, or for the rulers to relax, or to receive protection from bad treatment. Rather, the believers identify with the Lord's Messiah, ask God to fill them with supernatural boldness in the face of threats, and appeal to Him to continue performing "signs and wonders" (healings and other demonstrations of power), just as He had already been doing. In this way, the believers' prayer is both *militant* and *submissive*. They didn't wish harm on their enemies or take up arms against them— they simply prayed and committed the results to God. If they were hurt or died in the process, that was okay, because God was in control.

Luke states that after the believers prayed, the place where they were meeting was shaken and they were again filled with the Holy Spirit—just as had happened on the Day of Pentecost. This was a divine affirmation from God as a result of prayer, but it wasn't a guarantee that everything would be smooth or easy or without conflict. In fact, as Luke will record, it was just the beginning of the opposition they would face.

A Deadly Deceit

As previously noted, the members of the early Jesus movement shared their possessions with one another. In Acts 4:32-37, a man named Joseph—who will be better known in Acts as Barnabas—sells a field he owns and gives all the money to the church. This event does not go unnoticed by two other members of the church: Ananias and Sapphira.

The couple sees the attention Barnabas receives and decides to mimic his act—with one notable exception. They hold back a portion of the money they had received and then, to make themselves look good, deliberately deceive the church into believing they have given it all. Peter immediately recognizes the fraud and states to Ananias, "You have not lied just to human beings but to God" (Acts 5:4). At this, Ananias falls down and dies. Three hours later, Sapphira comes in and tells the same lie, and Peter gives the same pronouncement. She also falls down and dies. When the church hears about these events, great fear seizes them (see Acts 5:1-11).

The story of Ananias and Sapphira is one of the most difficult in Acts for modern readers to comprehend, as the couple's death appears to come about as a result of divine judgment for their sin. In many ways, what happened to Ananias and Sapphira is similar to what happened to Achan when the Israelites were on the threshold of entering into the Promised Land (see Joshua 7). Achan had also tried to deceive the people and the Lord, but his sin found him out. As Proverbs 9:10 and Psalm 111:10 state, "The fear of the LORD is the beginning of wisdom." This is what the story of Ananias and Sapphira is all about.

In telling this story, Luke is also warning us to guard against triumphal feelings that can come over us when we think things are going well—a belief that it is our own goodness or spirituality that is bringing blessings. This is superstition, not biblical thinking. It is pervasive among both believers and non-believers alike, but when it afflicts believers, it can be deadly. Seen in this light, it is actually an act of God's mercy that this event occurred when it did, as it prevented the believers in the new church from getting full of themselves and thinking they were better than others.

The Consequences of Numerical Growth

The Jesus movement was a growing movement not just in spirituality but also in measurable numbers. Numerical growth often correlates to signs and wonders, and this was certainly true of the Jesus movement. We can see this was the case by the progress reports that Luke intersperses throughout his narrative.

On the Day of Pentecost, Luke relates that 3,000 people believed (see 2:41). Two chapters later, Luke tells us that the number of men alone numbers 5,000 (see 4:4). In Acts 5:14, "more and more" come to believe as day after day, house to house and in the Temple, the disciples preach the gospel (see 5:42). The number of disciples rapidly increases, and many Jewish priests come to faith in Jesus (see 6:7). Later in Acts, Luke tells us that "many thousands of Jews" have believed (see 21:20).

God had prepared the soil, and the time was ripe. While these kinds of results are not automatic guarantees to anyone wanting to advance the gospel, they do set a standard. God wanted people to know Him and His Messiah, and day after day more and more people came to believe in Him.

QUESTIONS FOR PERSONAL APPLICATION AND DISCUSSION

In Acts 11:26, Luke refers to the members of the early Jesus movement as "Christians" for the first time. Interestingly, the Greek word used in this passage (*christianos*, "follower of Christ") has an ending that implies own-ership—Christians are "slaves" to Christ. In our culture, what does the name "Christian" mean to people you know?

_____

_____

_____

_____

_____

How did Jews tend to view members of the early Jesus movement? How did the early Roman historians view them?

_____

_____

_____

_____

_____

_____

What was the turning point in Rome's history that led to a change in attitude toward Christians? What was the result?

_____

_____

_____

_____

_____

According to Luke, what characteristics defined the Church in the days, weeks and months following its inception on the Day of Pentecost?

_____

_____

_____

_____

_____

How did the early believers view wealth? How is this different from what we see in some churches today?

_____

_____

_____

_____

What was the occasion that prompted Peter to deliver his second sermon to onlookers in Acts 3:11-26? How did Peter appeal to them and explain what was taking place?

_____

_____

_____

_____

What was the Jewish religious council's reaction to what had taken place? How did Peter and John respond? How did the believers then respond?

_____

_____

_____

_____

In Acts 5:1-11, Luke relates the story of Ananias and Sapphira. Why is this story often difficult for modern readers to comprehend?

_____

_____

_____

_____

_____

In what way were Ananias and Sapphira's actions like that of Achan in Joshua 7?

_____

_____

_____

_____

_____

What do you think Luke was warning believers to avoid by relating the story of Ananias and Sapphira?

_____

_____

_____

_____

As the gospel spread, more and more people came to believe in Christ and join the new Church. What consequences—both positive and negative—did this numerical growth bring?

_____

_____

_____

_____

_____

Notes

1. Publius Conelius Tacitus, *Annals*, book 15, chapter 44. This passage is one of the earliest non-Christian references to the origin of Christianity, the death of Christ, and the persecution of believers in the early Jesus movement.
2. Gaius Suetonius Tranquillus, *The Twelve Caesars*, "Claudius," book 25, chapters 1-5.
3. Ibid., "Nero," book 16, chapter 2.
4. Tacitus, *Annals*, book 15, chapter 44.

Sources

I. Howard Marshall, *The Acts of the Apostles: An Introduction and Commentary,* Tyndale New Testament Commentaries (Grand Rapids, MI: William B. Eerdmans, 1989), pp. 110-114.

Henrietta C. Mears, *What the Bible Is All About,* "Understanding Acts" (Ventura, CA: Regal Books, 2011), chapter 31.

Mears, *Highlights of Scripture, Part Four: Words and Works of Jesus, Teacher's Book* (Los Angeles, CA: The Gospel Light Press, 1937).

LIVING OUT LOUD
Dead to Self, Alive to God (Acts 5:12—7)

The death of Stephen and the connection between
witnessing and martyrdom.

KEY VERSE TO MEMORIZE

*I have been crucified with Christ and I no longer live, but Christ
lives in me. The life I now live in the body, I live by faith in the Son of God,
who loved me and gave himself for me.*
GALATIANS 2:20

WEEKLY READING

DAY 1	Matthew 24:36-51; 25:1-13; Luke 12:35-48; 17:20-37
DAY 2	Hebrews 12:1-3; Luke 24:44-59; Revelation 2:12-17; 17:1-6
DAY 3	Acts 5:12-42
DAY 4	Genesis 48; Psalm 60; Ecclesiastes 10:1-3; Matthew 25:31-41
DAY 5	Acts 6–7

FOR LEADERS: SESSION AT A GLANCE

SESSION OUTLINE	60 MIN.	90 MIN.	WHAT YOU WILL DO
Getting started	10	15	Pray and worship
Main points of the chapter	25	35	Discuss how Jesus is God's Word to us
Application and discussion	15	25	Discuss Stephen, the first martyr, and how witnessing and martyrdom are linked
Looking ahead	5	5	Prepare for next week
Wrapping up	5	10	Close with prayer or song

Martyrs and Witnesses

In this session, we're going to study Luke's account of Stephen, the Early Church's first martyr. However, before we get into Stephen's story, we first need to look at the interplay between the words "witness" and "martyr." Before we can do that, we need to understand *to whom* the disciples were (and we are!) supposed to witness. And before we can do that, we need to go back and review Jesus' last words to His disciples.

JESUS' LAST WORDS

In Matthew 28:18-20, the risen Jesus tells His followers to make disciples in every nation (Greek *ethne,* which refers to ethnic groups and families of peoples, not political nations). They are to baptize these followers "in the name of the Father and of the Son and of the Holy Spirit." Jesus promises He will be with them "to the very end of the age" (the end of history as we know it). This is called the Great Commission, because it is a command for *all* Jesus' disciples—wherever they are and in all times in history.

In Luke 24:36-48, the risen Jesus reminds His disciples that the Scriptures foretold that the Messiah must suffer and rise again on the third day and that "repentance for the forgiveness of sins will be preached in his name to all nations [*ethne*], beginning at Jerusalem." He then tells them, "You are witnesses of these things" and commands them to wait in Jerusalem for the promise of the Holy Spirit.

Then, in Acts 1, Jesus gives the same command (see verse 8). But just before He issues this command, the disciples ask a question that has troubled believers throughout the ages: "Lord, are you at this time going to restore the kingdom to Israel?" (verse 6). This was a reasonable inquiry, given that Jesus had claimed to be the promised Messiah and the resurrection had put God's stamp of approval on that claim. The problem was this: the Scriptures had painted two portraits of the Messiah that were difficult to put together. The first depiction of the Messiah was as a suffering servant who would die for the sins of people, taking the place of the old Mosaic sacrificial system (see Isaiah 53). The second depiction was as a conquering king who would vanquish the foes of God, establish peace on the earth and restore the kingdom of God (see Psalm 2).

We could rephrase the disciples' question this way: Now that Jesus had fulfilled part one of God's plan (His "First Coming"), would He fulfill part two of God's plan (His "Second Coming")? Jesus' two-part answer is terse: (1) They were not to speculate on when the end of the world will happen (see Acts 1:7), and (2) they were to be filled with the Holy Spirit so they could witness in all the world (Acts 1:8).

THE FUTILITY OF DATE-SETTING

Jesus' first statement in Acts 1:7-8 explicitly, concretely and absolutely forbids His followers from setting a date on the Second Coming: "It is not for you to know the times or dates the Father has set by his own authority" (Acts 1:7). This wasn't the first time Jesus had forbidden this kind of speculation. Earlier, He had said to His disciples, "But about that day or hour no one knows, not even the angels in heaven, nor the Son, but only the Father" (Matthew 24:36; Mark 13:32).

If what Jesus says is true that "no one" knows—not "the angels in heaven" or even the Son of God Himself, but *only* the Father—it should have settled this question for all time. But that's not what we see in the history of the Church. Time and again, Christians have ignored Jesus' command and put immense, near-obsessive efforts into determining the date of the Second Coming.

In one of the latest tries, a radio preacher put $100 million into a marketing campaign to convince people that May 21, 2011, would be the date of the "Rapture" (Christians being suddenly caught up from the earth) and that the end of the world would shortly follow. One atheist saw a business opportunity and offered an insurance policy to take care of peoples' pets if they were raptured—and some took him up on it. The date came and passed and nothing happened, so this preacher said he had "miscalculated" and that what really happened on May 21 was spiritual. Unfortunately, his "calculations" only served to bring mockery and disrepute on the gospel. The truth is that we are all accountable to God, that a judgment is coming, and that we need to be ready (see Matthew 22:8; 24:44; 25:10; Luke 12:35-40).

All attempts to predict the end of time have only served to point out three things about human nature: (1) the pride of some preachers runs deep, (2) religious people can be quite gullible, and (3) people aren't smarter than God. Furthermore, these Second Coming predictions have actually served to cause direct harm, as many have been duped into selling houses and off-loading their earthly goods in anticipation of an immediate journey to heaven. The reality we see in the Gospels and the book of Acts is that Jesus wants us to live in such a way that we are ready for His Second Coming to arrive at any time *because* we "do not know the day or the hour" (Matthew 25:13).

THE PRIORITY ON WITNESSING

Jesus' second statement in Acts 1:7-8 explicitly, concretely and absolutely commands His followers to be filled with the Holy Spirit so they can be witnesses to the gospel in every corner of the planet. The Greek word for "witness" that Luke uses in this passage, *marturoi* (the plural of *martus*), is employed three ways in the New Testament.

The first way is to describe a person who gives testimony in a court of law or a religious tribunal. In Jewish law, a person couldn't be condemned on the word of a single witness—the accusation had to be established by two or three others (see Deuteronomy 19:15; 2 Corinthians 13:1; 1 Timothy 5:19). In Matthew 26:65, when Jesus states in His trial before the Sanhedrin that He is the Son of God, Caiaphas, the high priest, says, "Why do we need any more witnesses?" In his view, Jesus had incriminated Himself. Later, in a perversion of the two- or three-witnesses principle, false witnesses testify against Stephen at his religious tribunal (see Acts 6:13). This first use of *martus* is not what Jesus was getting at in Acts 1:8. However, the next two uses do convey His intended meaning.

The second way that *martus* is used in the New Testament is to refer to someone who is an eyewitness to something. In Hebrews 12:1, the author likens the saints in heaven looking down on people's actions on earth to the *marturoi,* or spectators, at a sporting event. More often, however, *marturoi* is used to refer to those who experience the resurrected Jesus and, in turn, tell about Him to others. In Luke 24, after the risen Jesus gives His disciples a rundown of how He has fulfilled Messianic prophecies, He says, "You are witnesses of these things" (Luke 24:48). Shortly afterward, Jesus sends the Holy Spirit to empower His disciples to be "witnesses in Jerusalem, and in all Judea and Samaria, and to the ends of the earth" (Acts 1:8).[1]

The third way *martus* is used is to refer to a person who gives witness to Jesus and is killed for doing so. In Acts 22:20, Paul, praying to God, says, "When the blood of your martyr [*martus*] Stephen was shed, I stood there giving my approval and guarding the clothes of those who were killing him." In Revelation 2:13, the glorified Lord Jesus says to the church in Pergamum, "You did not renounce your faith in me, not even in the days of Antipas, my faithful witness [*martus*], who was put to death in your city." Also in John's apocalyptic vision, the mystical Great Whore of Babylon gets drunk on the blood of "those who bore testimony [*marturoi*] to Jesus" (Revelation 17:6).

We can see from these passages that all Christians are called to be witnesses (*marturoi*) to Christ and that some will have the privilege of being martyrs (*marturoi*) for Him. The way these terms intermingle in Greek shows that the early believers understood that witnessing for Christ could very well result in their death. This is exactly what happened to Stephen.

Renewed Persecution in the Church

The growth of the Jesus movement had not escaped the attention of the Jewish religious establishment. In Acts 5:17-18, they once again bring the apostles before the religious tribunal. This time members of the early Jesus movement are arrested and jailed.

For those of us living in Western societies, persecution represents a violation of a person's core civil rights and something not to be tolerated. The members of the Jesus movement had a different perspective. While persecution certainly wasn't pleasant, it wasn't regarded as strange or even unanticipated. In fact, the apostle Peter said that persecution was not only to be expected but also rejoiced in, because it allowed believers to take part in Christ's sufferings (see 1 Peter 4:12).

This apparent odd way of looking at suffering and persecution goes back to Jesus' Sermon on the Mount (see Matthew 5:11-12; Luke 6:22-23). In that teaching, Jesus braced His disciples for the hate crimes, insults, rejection, persecution and false accusations He knew would come as a result of their association with Him. He told them that rather than getting upset, they should rejoice because they knew there was a reward awaiting them in heaven.

A MIRACULOUS RESCUE

In this particular round of persecution the apostles are jailed, but during the night an angel of the Lord opens the doors and sets them free. The angel tells them to stand in the Temple courts and "tell the people all about this new life" (5:19). When the members of the Sanhedrin find out that the apostles are free, they round them up in the Temple court and have them again stand before the council. This ultimately leads to a flogging, after which the apostles rejoice "because they had been counted worthy of suffering disgrace for the Name [of Jesus]" (5:41).

Today, Christians who live in countries where there is great religious intolerance have a much better understanding of this principle than those who have grown up in places where freedom of religion is practiced.

In India, for example, believers encourage each other with the saying, "Any Christian should be ready at any time to preach, pray or die for Christ." They say this with a smile on their faces, but they mean it.

NEAR-MARTYRS

The Church of the second and third centuries made a distinction between those who were persecuted for their faith in Christ and didn't die (through harassment, imprisonment, fines, confiscation of property, beatings, torture and the like) and those who were put to death for their faith. The first were called "confessors," while the second were called "martyrs."

In Acts 5:29-40, Peter and John almost become the Church's first martyrs. After being brought before the Sanhedrin to give account for their actions (namely, preaching the gospel and healing in the name of Jesus), their answers so infuriate some of the members of the council that they want to put Peter and John to death (see verse 33). However, it is at this moment that Gamaliel, a respected teacher under whom the apostle Paul had studied (see Acts 22:3), provides a voice of reason.

Gamaliel mentions two other leaders of short-lived messianic movements—Theudas and Judas the Galilean—whose followers dispersed shortly after their deaths. He advises the council to pursue a course of caution and let the apostles go, reasoning, "If their purpose or activity is of human origin, it will fail. But if it is from God, you will not be able to stop these men; you will only find yourselves fighting against God" (verses 38-39). Gamaliel's speech persuades the others.

Luke wanted his readers to see Gamaliel's statement as being prophetic. In John's Gospel, Caiaphas had made a similar statement about Christ's death—that it would be better if one man died for the people rather than the whole nation perishing (see John 11:50; 18:14). In both cases, as the events unfold it is apparent that God is indeed with Jesus (God raised Jesus from the dead) and that God would indeed be with this new Jesus movement (which gathered steam and prospered despite persecution).

Dispute and Reconciliation

Following the persecution of the apostles, a dispute arises in Acts 6:1-6 that has the potential of causing major damage to the new movement. Apparently, some pre-existing friction exists between the Greek-speaking and Greek-influenced ("Hellenistic") Jews and the Hebrew-speaking and more traditional Jews. This erupts when the Hellenistic Jews complain that the Hebraic Jews are treating them unfairly in the daily distribution of food.[2]

The apostles' solution to the problem is not to ignore it or to offer a non-apology such as, "We regret if anyone was offended." In this they show wisdom, for such non-apologies (1) refuse to acknowledge that actual harm was done, (2) imply that the offense was entirely unintentional, (3) imply that taking responsibility for the offense is unnecessary, and (4) indicate that those who were offended were small-minded for doing so. Non-apologies are almost always dishonest dodges and are wholly ineffective in addressing real problems.

Instead, the apostles treat the situation seriously and responsibly. Because the charge is that the Greek-speaking widows are getting short-changed in the daily distribution of food, the apostles choose seven men who are full of the Holy Spirit and respected by all to oversee the process. Furthermore, the men they choose are Hellenistic Jews, as evidenced by their Greek names: Stephen, Philip, Procorus, Nicanor, Timon, Parmenas and Nicolas. With the Greek-speaking brothers in charge, no one could accuse them of favoritism toward the Hebrew-speaking widows.

The Church's First Martyr

Stephen was not the first person in the early Jesus movement to die, but he was the first to die for the sake of Jesus. For this reason, he is considered the Church's first martyr. Stephen, one of "the Seven" chosen to oversee the distribution of food to the Hellenistic widows, is a man full of faith, full of the Holy Spirit, and full of wisdom. God performs miracles through him, and a great number of Jewish priests come to faith in Jesus, presumably due in part to Stephen's witness.

Not everyone is happy with Stephen's Jews-for-Jesus, messianic Jewish movement. Some of the Jews try to oppose him in public, but they cannot answer Stephen's wisdom (see verse 10; see also Luke 21:15; Acts 4:13). So Stephen's opponents stir the people up against him and persuade some false witnesses to say, "We have heard Stephen speak blasphemous words against Moses and against God" (6:11).

This was not a light charge; it was extremely serious. The penalty for being convicted of speaking blasphemy carried with it a penalty of death— not by painless lethal injection, but by stoning. You can imagine the passions this would have ignited in the crowd at this moment.

THE CHARGES AGAINST STEPHEN

In Acts 6:13-14, the false witnesses charge: (1) that Stephen continually speaks against "this holy place" (Herod's Temple), and (2) that Stephen speaks "against the law" (the law of Moses as interpreted by custom and rabbis at the time). The evidence the witnesses produced was that Stephen had said Jesus would destroy the Temple and that Jesus would change the customs handed down by Moses.

Both charges contain a grain of truth. Jesus had not said that He would destroy the Temple, but that the time would come when "not one stone here will be left on another" (Matthew 24:2; Mark 13:2; Luke 21:6). This was a portion of a general prophecy that Jesus made against Jerusalem—a prophecy that came true in AD 70 when the Roman general Titus crushed a Jewish rebellion, reduced the city to ashes, and banished Jewish people from living anywhere near it. (Josephus writes about the terrible story of the siege and defeat of Jerusalem in *Wars of the Jews*.)

Regarding Jesus' changing the customs handed down by Moses, it is true that Jesus challenged some of the misinterpretations of Scripture (see Matthew 5–7) and some of the customs that went against the spirit of the law (see Mark 7:9-13 and the issue of *corban*, or what can be dedicated to God). Jesus also refuted the idea that some foods made people spiritually unclean, a notion based largely on the *kosher* laws of Leviticus 11 (see Mark 7:19). In fact, Jesus asserted His authority over interpretations of Mosaic law in ways that startled people (see Matthew 7:29; Mark 1:22).

To get to the heart of these charges requires Stephen to conduct a rabbinic, scholarly debate. That is exactly how he begins his defense.

STEPHEN'S DEFENSE

In Acts 7:1, the high priest asks Stephen, "Are these charges true?" At this point, Stephen begins his "apology" or defense before the Sanhedrin. The first portion of Stephen's speech in Acts 7:2-50 contains nothing the council hasn't heard before—just a basic rundown of the history of the Jewish people. There is hardly anything with which the members could disagree without really nitpicking, and there is certainly nothing remotely blasphemous to be found in Stephen's words.

In verse 37, Stephen hints that a Messianic prophecy refers to Jesus when he states, "This is the Moses who told the Israelites, 'God will raise up for you a prophet like me from your own people'" (quoting Deuteronomy 18:15). Peter had used this same passage in Acts 3:22 to show that

Moses had foretold that a "prophet like him" was coming, who was Jesus. In other words, the Messianic Jews for Jesus of the first century were saying that Jesus was their new Moses.

Making a statement like this would not have gone over well with traditionalist Jews. However, Stephen doesn't mention the name of Jesus at this obvious place. Instead, he starts hitting his hearers at a point they knew, from their own Scriptures, telling them that God had called the Israelites to account for their rebellion against God and God's prophets.

Then, in verses 51-53, Stephen abruptly changes tone. He calls the religious council "stiff-necked people" whose "hearts and ears are still uncircumcised." He accuses them of resisting the Holy Spirit and replicating the persecution of the prophets who predicted the coming of the Messiah. Stephen goes on to state that they have betrayed and murdered God's righteous Messiah Himself. The council is furious.

STEPHEN'S VISION
One of the more fascinating items in Scripture that is often overlooked by modern readers is the teaching on God's "right hand." In ancient times, a distinction was made between the right hand and the left. The right hand was considered a place of distinction and favor (see Genesis 48:13-19), a place of wisdom (see Ecclesiastes 10:2), and a place of power and strength (see Psalm 60:5). We see this distinction most clearly in Jesus' parable of the Sheep and the Goats, where He states, "When the Son of Man comes in his glory . . . He will put the sheep on his right and the goats on his left. Then the King will say to those on his right, 'Come, you who are blessed by my Father; take your inheritance. . . . Then he will say to those on his left, 'Depart from me, you who are cursed' " (Matthew 25:31,33-34,41).

The "right hand of God" is throne-room language. It is the place of intimacy with the divine King and the place of authority to carry out the divine will. Throughout Scripture, Jesus is depicted as sitting in this place of honor and power.

Psalms 2 and 110 show the Son of God sitting at God's right hand. In Luke 22:69, Jesus said of Himself, "From now on, the Son of Man will be seated at the right hand of the mighty God." During Peter's sermon on the Day of Pentecost, he said, "God has raised this Jesus to life. . . . Exalted to the right hand of God, he has received from the Father the promised Holy Spirit and has poured out what you now see and hear" (Acts 2:32-33).

Peter also stated before the Sanhedrin, "God exalted him [Jesus] to his own right hand as Prince and Savior that he might bring Israel to repentance and forgive their sins" (Acts 5:31).

After concluding his defense, Stephen looks up into heaven and sees a vision of the glory of God. "Look," he says, "I see heaven open and the Son of Man standing at the right hand of God." Notice that Stephen refers to Christ as "the Son of Man"—a title spoken by Jesus Himself that rarely appears outside of the Gospels (see Matthew 8:20; Mark 2:28; Luke 11:30; John 8:28; Revelation 14:14). In this way, Stephen sees Christ as the one who suffered and died and was vindicated by God, much as he will soon die at the hands of the religious leaders and be vindicated.

From the Sanhedrin's perspective, putting a man (Jesus) at God's own right hand was blasphemy, pure and simple. But that's not how the early believers saw it. They saw it as Jesus rising from His place of authority (notice that in Stephen's vision Christ is *standing* rather than *sitting*) to plead Stephen's case as an advocate before God and welcome him into God's presence (see Hebrews 7:25; 9:23-24; 1 John 2:1). Likewise, we can imagine Jesus rising whenever His people are persecuted for His name.

The outcome for Stephen is inevitable. Having been found guilty of blasphemy, the council begins to reign down stones upon him. As the rocks strike Stephen, he utters a prayer similar to the ones Jesus prayed on the cross: "Lord Jesus, receive my spirit" and "Lord, do not hold this sin against them" (Acts 7:59-60; see also Luke 23:34,46). If you study Christian martyrs through the ages, you will find many similar stories.[3]

QUESTIONS FOR PERSONAL APPLICATION AND DISCUSSION

The last words of a person are always important. In Jesus' case, His final words represented a command to all believers throughout all time. Why are Jesus' last words known as the "Great Commission"? How do we see the disciples carrying out this command so far in the book of Acts?

_____

_____

_____

_____

_____

_____

What are the two depictions of the Messiah in the Old Testament? How did this cause confusion among Jesus' disciples? How did Luke and members of the early Jesus movement explain these two different portraits?

_____

_____

_____

_____

What did Jesus say to His disciples about the timing of His return? Why is it futile to attempt to set dates for Christ's Second Coming? What danger does this create for Christians?

_____

_____

_____

_____

In what three ways is the term *martus* or *marturoi* used in the New Testament? What does this imply about how Jesus' followers were to approach witnessing for Christ to the world?

_____

_____

_____

_____

Why did Peter and John almost become the Church's first martyrs? Who saved them from death?

_____

_____

_____

_____

How did the apostles resolve the issue between Jewish and Gentile believers in Acts 6:1-6? How did their selection assure a resolution of the dispute?

_____

_____

_____

_____

In Acts 6:9 we read that opposition to Stephen arose "from members of the Synagogue of the Freedmen (as it was called)—Jews of Cyrene and Alexandria as well as the provinces of Cilicia and Asia." Why did Stephen come to the attention of this group? What did these groups of Jews do in order to bring changes against Stephen before the Sanhedrin (the Jewish ruling council)?

_____
_____
_____
_____
_____

What ultimately so infuriated the council and others present that they carried out the prescribed death penalty for blasphemy against God?

_____
_____
_____
_____
_____

The teaching that Jesus is now seated at the right hand of God relates to the ascension of Christ and is a major theme in the New Testament. Look up the following verses and write what each says about Jesus' role in this position at the right hand of the Father.

PASSAGE	JESUS' ROLE
Romans 8:34	
Hebrews 1:3	
Hebrews 1:13	
1 Peter 3:21-22	

Stephen lived his faith "out loud," meaning he was not afraid of living his faith publicly so that others could see it. How are you "living out loud" with your faith?

_____

_____

_____

_____

_____

If you're filled with the Holy Spirit, how much can God use you even if you're not "perfect" and "holy"?

_____

_____

_____

_____

_____

According to Galatians 2:20, when we decide to follow Christ, we die to self. This means that the threat of death has no effect on us because we're already "dead"—we've died in Christ and have been given the promise of eternal life. How might this knowledge help in persecution situations?

_____

_____

_____

_____

_____

Notes
1. Other uses of this meaning of *martus* can be found in Acts 2:32; 3:15; 5:32; 10:39,41; 13:31.
2. See session 7 for a more in-depth discussion of the difference between Hebraic Jews and Hellenistic Jews.
3. John Foxe (1517–1587), an English historian, captured many of these stories of Christian martyrs from the first to sixteenth centuries in his book *The Acts and Monuments* (published in 1563), which is more popularly known today as *Foxe's Book of Martyrs*.

Sources

I. Howard Marshall, *The Acts of the Apostles: An Introduction and Commentary,* Tyndale New Testament Commentaries (Grand Rapids, MI: William B. Eerdmans, 1989), pp. 148-149.

Henrietta C. Mears, *What the Bible Is All About,* "Understanding Acts" (Ventura, CA: Regal Books, 2011), chapter 31.

Mears, *Highlights of Scripture, Part Four: Words and Works of Jesus, Teacher's Book* (Los Angeles, CA: The Gospel Light Press, 1937).

NEAR FOREIGNERS
Philip, the Forerunner (Acts 8)

SESSION FOCUS

The spread of the gospel from Jerusalem to Judea, Samaria
and nearby foreign lands.

KEY VERSE TO MEMORIZE

For those who are led by the Spirit of God are the children of God.
ROMANS 8:14

WEEKLY READING

DAY 1	Acts 8
DAY 2	Luke 10:25-37; John 4
DAY 3	Isaiah 53
DAY 4	Psalms 68; 87
DAY 5	1 Corinthians 2

FOR LEADERS: SESSION AT A GLANCE

SESSION OUTLINE	60 MIN.	90 MIN.	WHAT YOU WILL DO
Getting started	10	15	Pray and worship
Main points of the chapter	25	35	Discuss how Jesus is God's Word to us
Application and discussion	15	25	Discuss how Philip was filled with the Holy Spirit, led by the Holy Spirit, and became a witness for Jesus
Looking ahead	5	5	Prepare for next week
Wrapping up	5	10	Close with prayer or song

The Gospel Moves Forth

As we have seen in this study, Acts 1:8 is the key to the book of Acts. It represents Jesus' last earthly command: "After he said this, he was taken up before their very eyes, and a cloud hid him from their sight" (1:9). It emphasizes the crucial importance attached to the promise the Father had made of sending the Holy Spirit: "You will receive power when the Holy Spirit comes on you" (1:8a). It introduces the term *martus*: "you will be my witnesses" (1:8b)—a term that broadens as the disciples move from being eyewitnesses to being obedient unto death. Acts 1:8 also establishes the storyline and literary structure of the book, charting how the gospel will move from Jerusalem to "all Judea and Samaria, and to the ends of the earth" (1:8c). Here's an outline of that structure:

SCRIPTURE	SETTING
Acts 1–7	Jerusalem
Acts 8–12	Judea, Samaria and nearby foreign lands (including Galilee, Ethiopia and Syria)
Acts 13–20	Faraway foreign lands (including Asia Minor, Crete, Macedonia and Greece)
Acts 21–28	Rome, the symbol of Gentile kingdoms and "the ends of the earth"

SETTING THE STAGE FOR THE PHILIP SAGA

At the end of Acts 7, Stephen utters a prayer of forgiveness for his persecutors as they throw stones at him (a form of capital punishment known as "stoning" or "lapidation"). Following this, he "falls asleep." Stephen is not dead; he is the first to see the glorified Jesus in heaven, who is standing up to receive him into heaven. It's as if Jesus is giving Stephen a standing ovation.

The men who killed Stephen are out of breath, flush from vanquishing a person they had judged to be a blasphemer. Nearby, a young man assigned to guard the cloaks of the witnesses watches in hearty agreement with what just took place. This young man's name is Saul (see Acts 7:58; 8:1).

Acts 7 marks the transition from the first major section of Acts (Jerusalem) to the second (Judea, Samaria and nearby foreign lands). Up to this point, all of the events depicted in Acts have occurred in and around Jerusalem among people who are almost 100 percent Jewish. Note that this does not mean 100 percent uniformity—the stories of Stephen and Philip depict a Jewish culture divided between Hellenistic Jews and Hebraic Jews. Let's consider this point in greater detail.

HEBRAIC AND HELLENISTIC JEWS

During the first century, Jewish people were either Hebraic Jews or Hellenistic Jews. This division had arisen at the time of Alexander the Great (356–323 BC), a warrior-king who conquered territory stretching from his homeland in Macedonia all the way to India. Alexander's tutor was Aristotle (384–322 BC), one of Greece's most famous philosophers.

Even before the time of Alexander, the Greek city-states were active colonizers in the Mediterranean Sea. The types of colonies the Greeks established generally took two forms: (1) Greek trading-colonies, and (2) independent city-states. When Alexander rose to power and began his conquest of the massive Persian Empire, he continued the spread of Greek language and culture (a process known as "Hellenization").[1] This included the land of the Jews.

For the Jews, there were many benefits that came with this spread of Greek culture, but there were also some major problems. Greek culture was pagan and included the worship of many gods, sexualized rituals in the pagan temples, and open nudity in the bathhouses and gymnasiums. As you can imagine, this created quite a bit of tension for the Jewish people, whose traditions were all about the worship of one God, keeping ritually pure, and sexual modesty.

The Jews found themselves with a choice: they could keep separate from Greek culture, or they could try to find ways to accommodate and adapt to it. The Jews who decided to keep separate came to be known as the Hebraic Jews. They drew a thick line between Jewish and Greek/pagan culture. They preserved their Hebrew language, read their Hebrew Scriptures, and kept Hebrew names. They maintained the special food laws that had been laid down by Moses, eating only "clean" foods and avoiding "unclean" foods (see Leviticus 11), and meticulously followed the other traditions in the Law. These are the ones who would have been happy to join along with Tevya in singing the song "Tradition" from *Fiddler on the Roof.*

The Hellenistic Jews, on the other hand, fuzzed up the line between Greek and Hebrew culture, or simply erased it. They went to Greek schools and learned to speak Greek, often losing contact with the Hebrew language of their ancestors in the process. Around 200 BC, this resulted in the creation of a Greek translation of the Hebrew Bible known as the Septuagint ("seventy," so named based on the tradition that it was constructed by 70 scholars). The Hellenized Jews gave their children Greek names (such as Stephen and Philip). They imbibed in Greek philosophy, enjoyed Greek food, and socialized with Greeks.

THE GREAT DIVIDE
From this we can see that by the time the Church was starting out, a significant divide existed between these two groups in Jewish culture. The Hebraic Jews would have seen the Hellenistic Jews as compromisers at best and traitors to the Mosaic tradition at worst. The Hellenistic Jews would have seen the Hebraic Jews as old-fashioned, tradition-bound and inflexible. This was no small division, and there is no difficulty imagining how these attitudes could have affected the Early Church.

We noted the first hints of this divide in session 6, when a complaint arose among the Hellenistic Jews that they were being treated unfairly by the Hebraic Jews (see Acts 6:1-6). Yet despite these difficulties and differences within the Jewish community, the Jewish believers in Acts 1-7 as a whole are those nearest to the promises of God and the biblical tradition. Now, as Luke moves into Acts 8, he turns the page from those who are "nearest" to Jerusalem to those who are "nearby."

Judea, Samaria and Nearby Foreigners
Those who are "nearby" include those living in Judea, Samaria and what we are calling the "nearby foreign lands." Of these, the people in Judea and Samaria are "near the nearest," with the next closest being foreigners in Galilee, Ethiopia and Syria.

Acts 8-12 represents the transition from the Early Church as a Messianic Jewish movement (with Jesus the Messiah being accepted by Hebraic and Hellenistic Jews) to a kind of haphazard, serendipitous moving of the gospel into the areas closest to Jerusalem. This section in Acts includes the remarkable stories of Philip the Deacon (Acts 8), the conversion of Saul (Acts 9), Cornelius and Peter's fateful meeting (Acts 10-11), and of another round of persecution (Acts 12). After Acts 12, the Church will move into a period of deliberate and sustained effort to reach out to the Gentile nations.

In Acts 8, Luke marks this shift by describing a multi-step process by which God gradually opens the eyes of the Early Church to its purpose to reach out cross-culturally to the world with the gospel.

Scattering by Persecution

Stephen's martyrdom in Acts 7 provided an example not only of a hero of the faith but also of a hero of the faith who didn't have a Hebraic Jewish background. Remember that *all* of Jesus' original disciples were Hebraic Jews. Stephen broke that mold.

After Stephen's death, a severe persecution breaks out against the Jesus movement in Jerusalem (see Acts 8:1). It's as if the stoning of Stephen was orchestrated to serve as the signal for the persecution to start. The Jews for Jesus are chased out of Jerusalem. This dislocation is undoubtedly painful, disconcerting and disorienting for them, but wherever they go they preach the gospel (see verse 4).

In a way, these early believers can't help themselves. They've experienced forgiveness in Jesus, healings and the hope of eternal life. Add to that the fact that the power of the Holy Spirit has come upon them—they've been baptized by fire and sent out by God. Witnessing is just going to happen.

The members of the early Jesus movement are scattered into Judea. In the Gospels, Jesus was born in Judea, and His southern ministry was in Judea. Judea is considered the Jewish heartland, located in the hill country—you "go up" to Judea and "come down" from there. The Jerusalem believers who landed in Judea were on home turf, even if if wasn't quite home.

The Samaritans

Some of the believers were also scattered into Samaria. As you may recall, the Samaritans and Jews didn't get along too well.[2] They both traced their religious traditions to Moses, but the Samaritans only accepted the first five books of the Bible. Meanwhile, the Jews' written tradition had expanded to include the rest of the books of the Hebrew Bible.

Despite these differences, Luke and Jesus had a soft spot in their hearts for the Samaritans. We can see this tenderness in Jesus' reaching out to the Samaritan woman at the well in John 4 and in His parable of the Good Samaritan (see Luke 10:25-37). In John 4, Jesus flips cultural expectations by talking openly to a woman of low reputation (holy men weren't supposed to do that) and refusing to get embroiled in a typical Jewish-Samarian controversy (about which mountain was the proper one on which to worship). In Luke 10, Jesus again flips cultural expectations, implying that the priest and the Levite are bad (not good) because they didn't help the poor traveler who had been attacked by robbers, while the Samaritan is good (not bad) because he showed compassion on the hurt man. At the end of the story, Jesus tells the Jewish expert in the law to go and be like the *Samaritan*.

In the Philip saga in Acts 8, Luke continues to show his sympathetic interest in Samaritans. Philip, like Stephen, was a Hellenized Jew, and in bringing the gospel to the despised Samaritans, he broke down a huge cultural barrier. Philip's example demonstrated to the Jewish church that God fully accepted the Samaritans and that they were acceptable as brothers and sisters in Christ. By spreading the gospel in Samaria, Philip also modeled how the message of Christ heals relationships and diffuses historic hatreds when it jumps from one culture to another.

PHILIP, A FORERUNNER TO PAUL

As mentioned in sessions 4 and 5, Philip is one of the men appointed by the Twelve to take care of widows' needs (see Acts 6:5). As a Hellenized Jew, Philip is not one of the true-blue Hebraic Jews, yet God uses him to reach out to the Samaritans. A lesson for cross-cultural missions here is that sometimes people will listen better to someone from a *different* culture than they will to one from a *similar* culture.

Philip doesn't just preach the gospel in word alone—he preaches with demonstrations of God's power that confirm the word of the gospel with signs and wonders. As a result, the Samaritans believe (see 8:8). Word soon gets back to the church in Jerusalem (the Hebraic Jewish apostles of Jesus) that through the ministry of Philip (yes, *Hellenistic* Philip), the Samaritans (yes, *those* Samaritans!) have put their trust in Jesus the Messiah.

Peter and John are dispatched to check things out and make sure everything is legit. When they arrive, Peter and John pray that the Samaritans might receive the Holy Spirit, as up to this point the Samaritans had only believed and been baptized. The Holy Spirit comes upon the Samaritans, *just as He came upon the Church on the Day of Pentecost* (see 8:14-17). It was a day of Holy Spirit power and paradigm shifting.

THE CONVERSION OF A NOTORIOUS SORCERER

In Deuteronomy 18:9-14, God had strictly warned the Israelites to have nothing to do with the occult. Despite this, a man named Simon had been practicing sorcery in Samaria for quite some time. Simon certainly didn't fit into the Jewish idea of holiness or righteousness—he was a man deep into magic and the occult. It would have been easy for the early believers to just write Simon off.

But the Lord uses Philip to open Simon's heart, and he is born again and baptized. God's work in Simon doesn't end there. Simon is something of a work in progress (as we all are). When Peter and John come to town, he sees the power of the Holy Spirit coming through the apostles' laying on of hands and prayer, and the old Simon wants a part of the action. He offers the apostles money and says, "Give me also this ability so that everyone on whom I lay my hands may receive the Holy Spirit" (verse 19). At this, Peter sternly warns Simon against trying to buy the gift of God with money. Simon repents, and the story ends happily (see verses 9-24).

In some cultures and subcultures, it took a notorious personality for the gospel to make a breakthrough. In this case, Simon—a famous sorcerer and magician—fit the bill. It also took a messenger with the courage to see the potential in everyone, including those who seem most opposed to the gospel. In this case, Philip fit that bill.

THE CONVERSION OF A NEARBY FOREIGNER

The next step in the spread of the gospel occurs in the story of Philip and the Ethiopian eunuch (see Acts 8:26-39). After spending time in Samaria, an angel of the Lord comes to Philip and tells him to travel south into Gaza. The journey from Ethiopia to Jerusalem and back again was about 1,000 miles, so Philip would have taken considerable time and gone to considerable expense to make the trip.

As Philip is walking south along the desert road, he meets an Ethiopian eunuch. Although Philip has traveled a great distance by this point, *culturally* this man is still a nearby foreigner. He is a Gentile, but he is also a God-fearer—a searcher after God whose quest had led him to get close to the Jewish community.

In fact, the eunuch had made the effort to attend a major Jewish religious festival. He also had in his possession a scroll containing the book of Isaiah, one of Israel's greatest prophets. For any foreigner to have a copy of Jewish Scripture was highly unusual. It would also have been a considerable hassle—scrolls were hand-copied on parchment (lamb skins sewn together), so they were large, heavy, bulky to carry around and extremely expensive.

It is evident God had already done a great deal of heart-preparation in this eunuch's life. When Philip encountered him, he was reading Isaiah 53, which is probably the most important verse used in sharing the gospel with Jewish people. Although it was written 750 years before Jesus' crucifixion, it perfectly describes what happened to Christ on the cross.

The Ethiopian asks a perceptive question: Was Isaiah speaking of himself or of someone else (see Acts 8:34)? Even the Ethiopian eunuch could see that this passage might point to "someone else" than Isaiah. So Philip explains to the eunuch, starting with the very passage from Isaiah 53:7-8 that the eunuch was reading, how it all connects to Jesus and the gospel.

From this we can discern three important principles. First, it is important to start with people where they are and move them toward a better understanding of the gospel. There is no formulaic approach that must be used for everybody—not everyone needs to hear the gospel in the same way. Second, sometimes God will prepare people's heart to hear the gospel, and they will be ready to receive Christ right then. We want to be ready for such moments. Third, the Holy Spirit is endlessly creative in how He works in peoples' lives. We want to try to keep ourselves aware of what the Holy Spirit is doing when we have conversations with people, whether they are people we know well or are complete strangers.

God had been working in both Philip's and the Ethiopian eunuch's lives to bring the two together. An angel of the Lord told Philip to take the road to Gaza, and a little while later the Holy Spirit told him to go to a particular chariot and stay by it (see Acts 8:26,29). Philip tells the gospel to the Ethiopian eunuch, and because God had been working in his heart, the Ethiopian believes and is baptized. He ultimately becomes the founder of the Church in Ethiopia.

QUESTIONS FOR PERSONAL APPLICATION AND DISCUSSION

The Jesus movement originally happened among Jesus, His 12 disciples and other men and women followers, almost all of them Hebraic Jews in Jerusalem. Based on the information in this session, what cultural barriers did this Jesus movement have to hurdle in order to become more widely known?

_____

_____

_____

_____

What were the two types of Jews at the time the Church was established?
In what ways were they similar? In what ways were they different?

_____

_____

_____

_____

_____

What happened to the early Jesus movement after the martyrdom of
Stephen? How did these events lead to Philip witnessing in Samaria?

_____

_____

_____

_____

_____

Philip, like Jesus, broke down many long-term cultural and religious barriers by sharing the gospel in Samaria. What were the results of his actions?

_____

_____

_____

_____

_____

What did Simon the Sorcerer do when he saw the power of the Holy Spirit
in Peter and John? How did Peter react?

_____

_____

_____

_____

How did God prepare the Ethiopian man's heart to receive the gospel?

_____

_____

_____

_____

How did God lead Philip to speak with the Ethiopian eunuch?

_____

_____

_____

_____

_____

_____

Read Isaiah 53. We can assume that the Ethiopian eunuch had been reading the entire chapter of Isaiah 53. We can also assume that the news of
Jesus' death (and the rumors among the Jews of His resurrection) had
been making the rounds in the conversations of those attending the Pentecost festival. How would this passage have spoken to the God-fearing
Ethiopian eunuch?

_____

_____

_____

_____

_____

Read Psalm 68:31 and Psalm 87:4 (note that in the Hebrew Bible, "Cush"
refers to Ethiopia). What was God's attitude toward the Ethiopians? How
does that relate to missions?

_____

_____

_____

_____

_____

_____

How was the Ethiopian eunuch's salvation a fulfillment of these ancient
prophecies?

_____

_____

_____

_____

_____

Think of the Christian group to which you currently belong. Do you see any "in-group" patterns that are limiting your group's ability to reach others with the gospel? If so, what could you do to help break down some of those barriers and get your people to reach out more?

_____

_____

_____

_____

_____

Do you think it is true that God always uses individuals (the human factor) to bring the gospel to others? Why or why not?

_____

_____

_____

_____

Read 1 Corinthians 2:1-5. There's always a danger in trying to replicate what the Holy Spirit does in somebody else's life, but what can you learn from Philip's experience about the filling, leading and motions of the Holy Spirit? What can you learn from Paul's experience?

_____

_____

_____

_____

_____

Notes

1. Incidentally, the adjective "Hellenistic" comes from Homer. Hellen, the mythical ancestor of the Greeks, was supposed to have come from Thessaly, from which his descendants, the "Hellas," spread out and formed the Greek-speaking states. See E. O. James, *Comparative Religion: An Introductory and Historical Study* (London: Methuen, 1938), p. 125.

2. For an explanation of the cause of the division, see session 9 in *The Life of Jesus* (Ventura, CA: Gospel Light, 2011) in the *What the Bible Is All About* Bible Study Series.

Sources

Henrietta C. Mears, *What the Bible Is All About,* "Understanding Acts" (Ventura, CA: Regal Books, 2011), chapter 31.

Mears, *Highlights of Scripture, Part Four: Words and Works of Jesus, Teacher's Book* (Los Angeles, CA: The Gospel Light Press, 1937).

WAS BLIND BUT NOW I SEE

An Amazing U-Turn (Acts 9:1-31)

SESSION FOCUS

The conversion of Saul, the persecutor of the early Jesus movement,
to Paul, the missionary to the Gentiles.

KEY VERSE TO MEMORIZE

*But the Lord said to Ananias, "Go! This man is my chosen instrument to proclaim
my name to the Gentiles and their kings and to the people of Israel."*
ACTS 9:15

WEEKLY READING

DAY 1	Acts 9:1-31
DAY 2	Acts 22:1-16; 26:1-18
DAY 3	Philippians 3
DAY 4	Galatians 1
DAY 5	Galatians 2

FOR LEADERS: SESSION AT A GLANCE

SESSION OUTLINE	60 MIN.	90 MIN.	WHAT YOU WILL DO
Getting started	10	15	Pray and worship
Main points of the chapter	25	35	Discuss how Jesus is God's Word to us
Application and discussion	15	25	Discuss Paul's conversion, its implications for Jews and Gentiles, and his significance in the early Jesus movement
Looking ahead	5	5	Prepare for next week
Wrapping up	5	10	Close with prayer or song

An Earth-Shattering Turn of Events

In the last session, we discussed how Philip, a Hellenistic Jewish believer in Jesus, got the ball rolling for cross-cultural outreach with his travels to Samaria and Gaza. We also discussed how Luke saw Philip as a forerunner to the apostle Paul, the one who really put cross-cultural missions on the map. In this session, we will examine the story of Paul's conversion and his work among Gentile believers.

THE SECOND MOST IMPORTANT PERSON IN WESTERN CIVILIZATION
Apart from Jesus, Paul is arguably the most important person in Western civilization. It is because of Paul that the Jews for Jesus Messianic movement broke out of the confines of Judaism and became more than just a sect of Judaism. It is because of Paul that Christianity expanded from the Middle East into Europe, where it ultimately influenced Western history, values, law, art, literature and music. And it is because of Paul that today—through 2,000 years of cross-cultural missions and cultural exchange—Christianity extends south into Africa, north and east into Russia and Asia, and in every direction to the island nations large and small. Notwithstanding the contributions of Philip in Acts 8 and Peter in Acts 10–11, it is primarily Paul who found a way to transcend cultural walls between Jews and Gentiles and translate the gospel so that the Gentiles could enthusiastically embrace it.

A HEBREW OF THE HEBREWS
Paul was born with the given name of "Saul." He grew up in Tarsus of Cilicia, a city located about 10 miles north of the Mediterranean Sea in what today is southern Turkey (see Acts 21:39). We don't know exactly when Paul was born, but given that he refers to himself in Philemon 1:9 as an "old man," and assuming that he was in his fifties or early sixties at the time, we can surmise that he was born sometime between 5 BC and AD 5. If this dating is correct, it would make him a contemporary of Jesus.

Luke states that though Paul was a "free-born" Roman citizen of Cilicia, he was raised in Jerusalem, where he studied under the famous teacher Gamaliel (see 22:3,28; 26:4). Paul himself says that he was circumcised on the eighth day (following tradition handed down from Abraham) and was "of the people of Israel, of the tribe of Benjamin, a Hebrew of Hebrews." He was from the strictest sect within Judaism (the Pharisees) and was thoroughly trained in Mosaic law (see Philippians 3:5-6). With regard to all things Jewish, Paul was *the man*.

Paul-as-Saul proved his loyalty to Judaism by persecuting members of the Early Church, who he believed were committing blasphemy by worshiping Jesus. In so doing, he could easily have justified his actions by appealing to passages such as Leviticus 24:16: "Anyone who blasphemes the name of the LORD is to be put to death. The entire assembly must stone them. Whether foreigner or native-born, when they blaspheme the Name they are to be put to death." As a zealous enforcer of Judaism, there was no way that Saul was going to let the Way prosper. He was going to snuff it out before it could cause any more damage than it already had.

A Dramatic U-Turn

Not content in rooting out believers in Jerusalem, Saul makes plans to seek out members of the Way in the Jewish communities in Damascus. Luke says that Saul went "to the high priest [Caiaphas] and asked him for letters to the synagogues in Damascus, so that if he found any there who belonged to the Way, whether men or women, he might take them as prisoners to Jerusalem" (Acts 9:1-2). The phrase "take them as prisoners to Jerusalem" doesn't tell the full story. According to Paul's own testimony, he "persecuted the followers of this Way to their death" (Acts 22:4) and "put many of the Lord's people in prison [where they] were put to death" (Acts 26:10).

Saul is a terrorist under legal cover. He is the leader of a death squad. When he later states that "Christ Jesus came into the world to save sinners—of whom I am the worst" (1 Timothy 1:15), he isn't exaggerating. He is personally responsible for the deaths of many men and women in the early Jesus movement, and humanly speaking, it is possible that he could have killed off the Church in its infancy. But this doesn't happen. As Saul is traveling to Damascus, something strange, surprising and wonderful takes place. The resurrected Jesus meets him along the road and speaks to him by name, saying, "Saul, Saul, why do you persecute me?" (verse 4).

Luke gives a third-person account of the story in Acts 9:3-22, and he later cites Paul's first-person account in Acts 22:1-14 and 26:1-18. Saul's conversion story is compelling on its first telling, and the fact that Luke mentions it three times in Acts emphasizes just how earth-shattering it truly was for the Early Church. It was certainly earth-shattering for Saul— the encounter completely changes the course of his entire life. But not right away, because first Jesus blinds Saul in a flash of light from heaven.

PROPHECY AND PRUDENCE

After blinding Saul, Jesus tells him to get up and go into Damascus, where he will receive further instructions. Then He gets other people involved to confirm the message. At about the time Jesus is confronting Saul, He appears in a vision to a man named Ananias (not the same Ananias as in Acts 5) and gives him some specific instructions to find Saul "on a Street called Straight" (Acts 9:11, *KJV*).

At first, Ananias is less than pleased with the instruction. He protests to Jesus, saying, "Lord . . . I have heard many reports about this man and all the harm he has done to your holy people in Jerusalem" (verse 13). In other words, "Lord, this man is dangerous!" But Jesus replies, "Go! *This man is my chosen instrument to proclaim my name to the Gentiles* and their kings and to the people of Israel. I will show him how much he must suffer for my name" (9:15-16, emphasis added).

While Ananias gets only a short mention here and in Acts 22 and 26, the impact of this one man listening to the voice of the Lord has reverberated throughout the ages. Despite his fear, he follows Jesus' command and prays for Saul to see again and to be filled with the Holy Spirit. Then he connects Saul to the brothers and sisters in Damascus. And the rest, as they say, is history.

Well, actually the story has more twists and turns than that. Not too long after Saul's conversion, he begins preaching in Damascus. He baffles those who try to argue against him and proves to them that Jesus is the Messiah. Then, after "many days had gone by" (Acts 9:23), a conspiracy arises to kill Saul. Saul could have stayed visible, preaching in the open, trusting God to preserve his life. But prudence prevails, and the disciples help him escape by lowering him down in a basket from the city wall.

A short time later, Saul arrives in Jerusalem. The apostles there are justifiably suspicious—they had been betrayed once (by Judas), and they aren't going to easily fall for a treacherous trap. But one of the believers, named Barnabas (the same Barnabas mentioned in Acts 4:32-37), concludes that Saul's conversion is on the up and up, and he vouches for him before the apostles. Again Saul preaches boldly, again a group plots to kill him, again the believers learn of the plot, and again prudence prevails and Saul is hurried out of the city. The believers in Jerusalem take Saul down to the docks in Caesarea and put him on a boat headed to his hometown in Tarsus, where they believe he will be safe for the time being (see 9:23-31).

In both of these escapes, we don't hear of any prophetic warnings. We only hear of the disciples catching on to the plots and coming up with some good, solid, common-sense responses. In this, it's important to see that God uses both *supernatural* and *natural* means to get the job done. Just because the means are natural doesn't mean they aren't providential. The bottom line is that God works through people, and it's not always predictable or "evenly spaced" as to how God is going to work.

SAUL, WHO WAS ALSO PAUL

Luke refers to Saul by his given birth name up until Acts 13:9, where he abruptly states that Saul is "also called Paul." From this point on, Luke refers to him consistently as "Paul," only referring to Saul in retrospect in Acts 22:7,13 and 26:14. In truth, as a Roman citizen Paul would have had three names, the third of which (his *cognomen*) would have been the Latin name "Paullus" ("Paulos" in Greek). Given this, by switching from "Saul" to "Paul," Luke is implying that Paul was now entering into the Gentile phase of his ministry.

In the Bible, we find a recurring tradition of God renaming people when He reveals their life work or their true character to them. For example, in Genesis 17:5, God changes Abram ("father") to Abraham ("father of a multitude"). In Genesis 32:28, after an all-night wrestling match, He changes Jacob ("usurper") to Israel ("prince of God"). Later, in the New Testament, Jesus changes Simon ("obedient") to Peter ("the rock"), and says to him, "On this rock I will build my church, and the gates of Hades will not overcome it" (Matthew 16:18).

Something similar happened with Saul. Technically, God didn't rename him—he was merely called by two names: Saul and Paul. Saul is a Hebraic Jewish name, and as such it would have reflected his Jewish heritage and culture. Saul was rightfully proud of this name that his parents had given him. However, when Jesus met Saul on the road to Damascus, He gave him a new mission in life: to be the apostle to the *Gentiles*. Rather than allowing his Hebraic name to become a needless stumbling block to Gentiles, and to better identify with them, Saul began using his Greek name. Eventually, his Greek name overtook his Hebrew name, and "Paul" stuck.

Using a Greek name was a big cultural leap on Saul's part. One of the biggest imperatives within Judaism was to be separate, to "come out from" the Gentiles, and to not allow oneself to become polluted by Gentile uncleanness. Saul's willingness to change his name to Paul—even temporarily and only when he might have been visiting Gentile towns—was one of many changes he was willing to make to be more open, more available, more accessible to and more effective with the Gentiles. It was a big concession, but a concession for a higher purpose: the advancement of the gospel.

A Polarizing Figure

As previously noted, Paul is an incredibly important figure in Western history. For this reason, he is also a controversial and even polarizing figure. To understand why this is the case, we need to dig beneath the surface to understand who Paul really was and the significance of his contributions to the Early Church.

PAUL AS AN AUTHOR OF SCRIPTURE

As Luke records in the book of Acts, Paul founded a number of Christian communities throughout the Mediterranean region. To keep in touch with these believers as he traveled from place to place, Paul wrote a series of letters to instruct them on certain points of doctrine that he had heard they were not following, or to encourage them in their faith, or to provide them with specific instructions. This is significant, because 13 of these letters on which his name appears still survive—Romans, 1 and 2 Corinthians, Galatians, Ephesians, Philippians, Colossians, 1 and 2 Thessalonians, 1 and 2 Timothy, Titus and Philemon—and many believe he also wrote or was the seminal thinker behind the book of Hebrews.[1] This makes Paul a major player in the formation of the New Testament canon.[2]

In the early Jesus movement, the only Bible the believers had was the Hebrew Bible, or the Old Testament. They also had the testimony of many of the original 11 disciples who were with Jesus, and their words carried much weight, but the New Testament as a recognized body of Scripture did not yet exist. What this means is that at the time the Church was being birthed and growing in its early years (the period covered by the book of Acts), the Gospels of Matthew, Mark, Luke and John, the letters of Paul, and the other New Testament writings were being composed.

Because the early Jesus movement was a messianic Jewish movement, believers modeled their worship meetings after worship meetings in Jewish synagogues. They prayed, sang hymns and read passages from the Hebrew Bible, the authoritative Scriptures for the Jewish people. What is remarkable is how the early Jesus movement added explicit Jesus-worship elements to their worship. They created hymns (as quoted in 1 Timothy 3:16) and, as the Gospels and letters of Paul, Peter and John were being hand-copied and circulated to the churches, began to read portions of these texts out loud at their assemblies.

In this way, Paul's letter to one church became a message not just for that specific community of believers but also for *all* believers in the Body of Christ. The same was true of the other letters. The important point to understand is that the churches recognized Paul's letters (along with the other New Testament writings) as having the Holy Spirit's stamp of life-changing authority—*and as having the same God-inspired authority as the Hebrew Bible* (see 1 Timothy 3:16-17; 2 Peter 3:15-16). The independent churches scattered across the Roman Empire gradually recognized certain collections of writings as authoritative Scripture as they used them in worship, put them into practice, and saw their effectiveness in changing people's lives for the better.

PAUL THE APOSTATE?

The Jewish people who did not accept Jesus as Messiah considered Paul a traitor and an apostate (somebody who rejects and teaches against the religion he or she grew up in). They claimed Paul was negating the Laws of Moses, the Scriptures and the core of their tradition. In reality, in none of Paul's writings did he ever reject the Old Testament, or say that it was in error, or even claim that the Jewish people had corrupted their own Scriptures. Rather, Paul (and the other New Testament writers) affirmed the validity and enduring value of the Old Testament.

However, Paul did say that the gospel had *superseded* the Old Testament. The reason for this was because Jesus' coming to the earth had fundamentally changed things, and what had been done in the past could no longer be practiced in the future. Judaism had focused on one God, but Jesus claimed to be one with God and to be God's Son—a fact that required a lot of rethinking for traditionalist Jews. Judaism had been a Temple-oriented religion, but Jesus' sacrifice on the cross made the need for sacrifices at the Temple obsolete (see Hebrews 8-10). Judaism had been intensely focused on fidelity to Mosaic law, but Jesus didn't always conform to Mosaic law (in the ways Jewish people might have wanted Him to do), and sometimes He acted as if Mosaic law was already on the way out (see Matthew 5-7).

In addition, Paul's take on what it meant to be a Jew and the role of the Mosaic law in spiritual life were at odds with prevalent Jewish thinking at the time. Paul taught that a person was a genuine Jew not by birth but by his or her heart attitude toward God and Jesus (see Romans 2:17-29). Paul also taught that the Mosaic law had no power to make a person good; in fact, the only power it had was to reveal a person's sin to him or her (see Romans 7–8). In this way, Paul put the law of God and the promise of God in tension with each other so that people could see their need for God's grace.

Seen in this light, Paul was not an apostate Jew at all—he was just a Jewish believer in Jesus. Like other Jewish believers, he considered himself to be a "completed" Jew because he believed in God's promises of the coming Messiah that had been fulfilled in Jesus' arrival. To Paul, believing in God's Messiah was not apostacy!

PAUL AND THE LAW

Paul's theology (the way he pulled together Scripture, reason and experience into a comprehensive understanding of God) centered on God's promises—which, it could be strongly argued, was exactly what Jesus taught. Jesus wasn't about following the minutiae of the 613 laws of Moses or the additional customs that had been added to Scripture by Jewish tradition. In fact, Jesus used the same kind of critique of rules-following that is found in the greatest prophets of Israel. To try to drive a wedge between genuine Judaism and Paul is thus like trying to drive a wedge between genuine Judaism and Jesus. It can be attempted, but it will never be successful.

When it came to defining the purpose of the law, Paul's overriding principle was that it compelled people to recognize their sin and the depths of God's grace. For Paul, it was overweening pride and folly for people to believe they could earn God's favor and save themselves through their works or good deeds. This is actually a message that is carried throughout the Hebrew Bible, beginning in Genesis 15:6, where God reckoned Abraham's faith in God's promises as righteousness, and continuing all the way through the history of Israel, the teachings of the prophets, and up to Jesus.

In the end, Paul's mission (given to him directly by Jesus) was to translate the message of Christ into a "language" the Gentiles could understand. For this reason, Paul couldn't very well preach the gospel of freedom in Christ and then demand Gentiles to conform to all the rigors of Jewish tradition, as doing so would be giving two contradictory messages. Instead, Paul successfully navigated between honoring the old while boldly proclaiming the new. This might have been threatening to the old guard and their way of looking at things, but it was not apostacy.

QUESTIONS FOR PERSONAL APPLICATION AND DISCUSSION

Why could Paul arguably be described as "the second most important person in Western civilization"?

_____

_____

_____

_____

_____

_____

Why did Paul's conversion represent a dramatic turn of events both for early Christians and for those in the Jewish establishment?

_____

_____

_____

_____

_____

Ananias was not a "head honcho" in the Early Church, but he got a clear message from God. What role did he play in bringing Saul into the body of believers? What does this say about the type of person God chooses to do His will?

_____

_____

_____

_____

_____

What is the connection between "prudence" and "prophecy" in Paul's early escapes from attempts on his life? Was God at work in the believers' prudent attempts to save Paul?

_____

_____

_____

_____

_____

What was the significance of Saul's name change to Paul? Do you think it was hypocrisy for him to use two names in this way? Are there any situations in your life where you have used different "names" to address different groups of people?

_____

_____

_____

_____

_____

_____

What is significant about the fact that the early believers copied and passed Paul's letters along to other churches? How did this lead to him becoming the author of most of the New Testament?

_____

_____

_____

_____

_____

_____

Why did the Jews who did not accept Jesus consider Paul to be an apostate? Was this a valid claim? Why or why not?

_____

_____

_____

_____

_____

What did Paul say *had* changed since the coming of Jesus to the earth? What types of things under the Old Covenant were no longer applicable under the New Covenant?

_____

_____

_____

_____

_____

According to Paul, what was the overriding purpose of the law? Is this a different viewpoint from what we see in the Old Testament? Why or why not?

_____

_____

_____

_____

_____

Why would Paul's mission to the Gentiles—given to him directly by Jesus—have made it impossible for him to enforce the rules of Jewish tradition?

_____

_____

_____

_____

Conversion has three directions: (1) to God, (2) to the Church, and (3) to the world. How did each of these take place in Saul's conversion story? How did they take place in your conversion story?

TO GOD	TO THE CHURCH	TO THE WORLD
Paul's story		
Your story		

Notes

1. This is not to say that scholars are in agreement that Paul was the actual author of all of these letters. Typically, letters attributed to Paul fall into three categories: (1) "Undisputed" letters (Romans, 1 and 2 Corinthians, Galatians, Philippians, 1 Thessalonians and Philemon); (2) "Debated" letters (Ephesians, Colossians, 2 Thessalonians); and (3) "Doubtful" letters (1 and 2 Timothy, Titus).

2. A "canon" (from the Greek *kanon,* meaning "rule" or "measuring stick") is an authoritative body of Scripture (there is also an Old Testament canon). While there were many ancient canons compiled, the list we have today comes from an Easter letter written by Athanasius, Bishop of Alexandria, in AD 367. The Council of Carthage accepted this list in AD 397 under the authority of Augustine of Hippo.

Sources

I. Howard Marshall, *The Acts of the Apostles: An Introduction and Commentary,* Tyndale New Testament Commentaries (Grand Rapids, MI: William B. Eerdmans, 1989), pp. 166-169.

Henrietta C. Mears, *What the Bible Is All About,* "Understanding Acts" (Ventura, CA: Regal Books, 2011), chapter 31.

Mears, *Highlights of Scripture, Part Four: Words and Works of Jesus, Teacher's Book* (Los Angeles, CA: The Gospel Light Press, 1937).

L. Michael White, *From Jesus to Christianity* (New York: Harper Collins, 2003), pp. 145-147.

THE STRANGE SHEET
What God Says Is Clean Is Clean (Acts 9:32–12)

SESSION FOCUS

A strange vision breaks down barriers between Jewish and Gentile believers in the early Jesus movement.

KEY VERSE TO MEMORIZE

But God has shown me that I should not call anyone impure or unclean.
ACTS 10:28

WEEKLY READING

DAY 1	Matthew 9:25; Luke 7:11-17; John 11:1-44; Acts 9:32-43
DAY 2	Leviticus 11–12; 15; Numbers 19
DAY 3	Acts 10
DAY 4	Acts 11
DAY 5	Acts 12

FOR LEADERS: SESSION AT A GLANCE

SESSION OUTLINE	60 MIN.	90 MIN.	WHAT YOU WILL DO
Getting started	10	15	Pray and worship
Main points of the chapter	25	35	Discuss how Jesus is God's Word to us
Application and discussion	15	25	Discuss how Peter's vision illustrates the key conflict in the book of Acts and what it teaches about breaking down walls of fear and hatred
Looking ahead	5	5	Prepare for next week
Wrapping up	5	10	Close with prayer or song

Now Back to Peter

In the last session, we saw an example of clear, unambiguous prophecy when Jesus spoke to Ananias in a vision and told him to pray for Paul. In this next section in Acts, we will encounter an example of bizarre, head-scratching prophecy. Ultimately, this prophecy will be deciphered and lead to the gospel breaking out among the Gentiles.

MIRACLES FOLLOW PETER

We haven't heard anything from Peter for a while. Now, at the end of Acts 9, after the spectacular conversion of Saul-who-will-also-become-known-as-Paul, the spotlight again returns to the early Jesus movement's undisputed first leader. Peter might have taken the easy route of playing the big shot and waiting for people to come to him in Jerusalem. But that's not what he does. Rather, he itinerates around, traveling from place to place where belief in Jesus as the Messiah was popping up in Judea, Galilee and Samaria. Peter strengthens the believers in these groups with teaching and encouragement, and as he goes, he heals people in the name of Jesus through the power of the Holy Spirit. These miracles open the hearts of people.

One of the places Peter travels is the town of Lydda (modern-day Ludd), where he meets a man named Aeneas. This follower of Christ had been confined to his bed for eight years. When Peter sees him, he says, "Jesus Christ heals you. Get up and roll up your mat" (Acts 9:34). Aeneas immediately gets up, and when the people in the area see him walking around, many of them turn to the Lord (see Acts 9:32-35).

Another miracle occurs in the town of Joppa (current-day Jaffa, located south of Tel Aviv in Israel). A woman there named Tabitha, also known as Dorcas (her Greek name), was well known for her compassion for the poor and her good deeds. She had died, her body had been washed and covered with linen in anticipation of her burial, and the women mourners were wailing. When Peter shows up, he follows the pattern of Jesus by ushering them out of the room (see Matthew 9:25; Luke 7:11-17; John 11:1-44), prays, and tells her to get up. Tabitha opens her eyes, and Peter presents her to the other believers. The news of her resurrection spreads in her hometown and many people come to believe in the Lord (see Acts 9:40-42).

DEAD THINGS

That night, Peter stays at the house of a tanner by the name of Simon. The fact that Peter ends up staying at his house is interesting on several levels.

First, both men have the same name (Simon-Peter and Simon-the-tanner). Second, they both have Hebraic Jewish names, which indicates they had a lot in common religiously and culturally. Third, Simon's occupation of making animal skins into leather meant that he was constantly in contact with dead animals. In Jewish culture, touching a dead animal—even if it was considered ritually clean (an animal that could be eaten according to Jewish dietary laws)—made one unclean for the rest of the day. This meant that every working day, Simon put himself into a state of ritual impurity that went on until that ritual impurity could be lifted.

Ritual purity was not some trivial item in Jewish law. If you were ritually unclean, you were effectively "cut off" from worship with the rest of the community. You weren't allowed to enter the Temple to pray, worship or sacrifice until (1) a prescribed length of time had passed, and (2) you had taken a ritual bath in a special ritual cleansing place (known as a *mikvah*).

The Law of Moses detailed how many days various kinds of ritual uncleanness would last (see Leviticus 11–12; 15; Numbers 19). These regulations were to be strictly followed. For tanners, the relevant law is found in Leviticus 11:39-40: "If an animal that you are allowed to eat dies, anyone who touches its carcass will be unclean till evening. Anyone who eats some of its carcass must wash their clothes, and they will be unclean till evening. Anyone who picks up the carcass must wash their clothes, and they will be unclean till evening."

So, while Simon Peter was staying at Simon the tanner's house, there would have been ample opportunity for him to observe and talk about issues having to do with cleanness and uncleanness. Ritual purity was always on the minds of those in Jewish culture, but Simon Peter was now very close to the day-to-day impact of that law on tanners.

A Strange Vision

Meanwhile, in the city of Caesarea, located about 30 miles away from Joppa, there lived a military officer named Cornelius. Caesarea was a port city that had been constructed by King Herod the Great in 22 BC to curry favor with the then-ruling Roman emperor Caesar Augustus. It was a thoroughly Roman city, complete with storerooms, markets, baths, temples to Roman gods and various public buildings. Cornelius was a Roman officer who was stationed there as part of the Italian Regiment of the Roman occupying army. With the rank of centurion, he commanded a force of about 100 men.

CORNELIUS, THE GOD-FEARER

Cornelius was not a Jew, but he and his whole family were devout God-fearers. As Gentiles, they had firmly attached themselves to the Jewish community in Caesarea. Cornelius gave generously to those in need and prayed regularly. On this day, he was praying at "the third hour," after noon, the Jewish hour of prayer.

As Cornelius is praying, an angel comes to him in a vision and says, "Your prayers and gifts to the poor have come up as a memorial offering before God" (Acts 10:4). A "memorial offering" was a food offering that produced "an aroma pleasing to the LORD" (Leviticus 2:2,9). The angel, in effect, was telling Cornelius that God was pleased with his life. The angel then tells him to send couriers to Joppa to bring back a certain person. The angel makes it clear who this individual is and where he will be found: "Send men to Joppa to bring back a man named Simon who is called Peter. He is staying with Simon the tanner, whose house is by the sea" (Acts 9:5-6).

KILL AND EAT

In this story, timing is everything. About noon the next day, Peter is praying on the roof of Simon the tanner's house. Peter is waiting for a meal, and as he is praying the smells of the cooking waft up from below. Peter falls into an altered state of consciousness (maybe he was *really* hungry), and he has a vision of heaven opening. Then God shows Peter a strange sight: something like a sheet lowers to earth filled with all kinds of animals: four-footers, reptiles and even birds. Then something even stranger happens. A voice commands, "Get up, Peter. Kill and eat" (Acts 10:13).

Peter had grown up Jewish and since his youth had followed the Mosaic food laws (see Leviticus 11). So, understandably, he tells the Lord that he can't "kill and eat" because there are unclean animals on that sheet—he's never eaten unclean food, and he doesn't intend to start now. Then the voice contradicts him, saying, "Do not call anything impure that God has made clean" (verse 15). This happens three times, and then the sheet is pulled back into heaven.

THE KEY TO ACTS

We previously noted that Luke tells the story of Paul's conversion three times in Acts, which serves to emphasize that it is really important. Luke tells the strange sheet story *six* times. If Paul's conversion deserves big, bold headlines, the strange sheet story deserves bigger, bolder headlines, plus multiple exclamation points. We could almost say that the strange sheet is the key to the whole book of Acts. But if this is true, what does the vision actually signify?

To determine this, we need to leave Peter pondering what he has seen in his heart and discuss the Law of Moses. God's purpose for the Mosaic Law was to create a separate, pure and distinct people—a people to demonstrate God's glory and His name (see Exodus 9:16). To that end, the Mosaic Law had four parts: (1) the moral law (summarized in the Ten Commandments); (2) the social laws (laws governing social relationships); (3) the laws of ritual purity (the food laws were part of the dynamic of clean/unclean); and (4) the sacrificial laws (the laws about animal sacrifices and the Temple).

JESUS AND MOSAIC LAW

Whereas Mosaic Law bundled these into an inseparable package, Jesus broke them out and separated them. On the moral law, Jesus was uncompromising. He fully affirmed the Ten Commandments (the foundation of Mosaic Law), though on one of the commandments—the one about keeping the Sabbath—He had a different take than most Jews. In the Old Testament, doing any work on the Sabbath could get a person killed (see Exodus 31:14-15). However, Jesus healed on the Sabbath, and His disciples picked heads of grain, both of which were considered "work." When the Pharisees questioned Him about this, He said, "The Sabbath was made for man, not man for the Sabbath" (Mark 2:27). In this way, Jesus set aside a super-strict interpretation of doing absolutely no work on the Sabbath.

Regarding the social laws, Jesus focused on the broad principles—what He called "the weightier provisions of the law: justice and mercy and faithfulness" (Matthew 23:23, *NASB*). To Him, these were more important than meticulous tithing of "mint, dill and cumin." On the laws of ritual cleanness and uncleanness, Jesus wasn't such a stickler. Long before Peter's vision in Acts 10, Jesus had already set aside the Mosaic food laws (see Matthew 15:11; Mark 7:15; compare with Paul's words in 1 Timothy 4:3-5). And on the Old Testament sacrificial laws, Jesus fulfilled them in such a way that the shedding of the blood of bulls, goats and lambs was no longer necessary.

In diverging from the traditionalist interpretation of Moses, Jesus was a taboo-breaker. His actions set in motion a change in how people viewed Old Testament law. Similarly, when Peter started mingling with Gentiles and eating unclean food, he was also a taboo-breaker. Both Jesus' and Peter's objective was not to thumb their nose at God's law, but to fulfill it in the deepest sense.

PIECING THINGS TOGETHER
In the midst of Peter's pondering, the Holy Spirit tells him that three men have just arrived at the house and that they are looking for him. The men tell Peter about Cornelius, Peter invites them to stay the night, and the next day they walk to Cornelius's house. Cornelius's household (his family, servants and paid laborers who served the family) and a large group of Cornelius's close friends and relatives—all Gentiles—are waiting to hear what Peter has to say.

Peter begins by acknowledging the uncomfortable cultural bind in which he finds himself: Jews aren't supposed to mingle with Gentiles or even visit them. However, he tells them, "God has shown me that I should not call anyone impure or unclean" (Acts 10:28). (He had previously backed up these words by inviting Cornelius's messengers into Simon the tanner's home and sharing a meal with them.) Peter's statement is a great leap forward for the gospel and for humankind, as it throws out the notion that Gentiles are inferior. It represents the first step in overthrowing feelings of cultural superiority that are such poison to the advancement of the message of Jesus in the world.

An Astonishing Turn of Events
If you want to know the unvarnished gospel—the message the early Jesus movement preached—Peter articulates it with crystal clarity in Acts 10:34-43. Peter had not even finished his talk when the Holy Spirit comes powerfully on this entire Gentile group, *just as He had come upon the earliest Jewish believers on the Day of Pentecost* (see Acts 10:47). This outpouring of the Holy Spirit completely blows the minds of the "circumcised believers"—the Jews for Jesus who had come with Peter to Cornelius's house. It had never even entered their heads that such a thing could happen.

BAPTISM AND THE HOLY SPIRIT
When Peter sees the Gentiles speaking in tongues and praising God, he says, "Surely no one can stand in the way of their being baptized with water. They have received the Holy Spirit just as we have" (Acts 10:47). This

issue as to who could be baptized is one that actually comes up frequently in the story of the early Jesus movement.

In the Jewish tradition, immersion in water (Greek *baptismos*) was a form of purification for those who had become defiled and "unclean," such as by coming into contact with a dead body (see Numbers 19:11-20). Over time, the Jews had adopted the custom of baptizing proselytes (those on the way to adopting the Jewish faith) seven days after they were circumcised. During the baptism, the proselyte was immersed in water, and when the individual rose he or she was considered a true member of Judaism. After baptism, the person was allowed access to the sacrifice in the Temple.

Baptism thus represented a change in status—an idea that John the Baptist adapted in his teaching of the coming Messiah.[1] The Early Church took this concept one step further. Jesus had said, "Truly I tell you, no one can enter the kingdom of God unless they are born of water and the Spirit" (John 3:5), and they understood baptism in water to be *intimately connected* to "baptism by fire"—a poetic way of talking about being filled with the Holy Spirit. This is exactly what John the Baptist had predicted and what Jesus had promised (see Acts 1:5; 11:15).

We see this connection throughout the book of Acts. In Peter's first sermon, he told his listeners to "repent and be baptized . . . and you will receive the gift of the Holy Spirit" (2:38). When Philip preached the gospel in Samaria, he baptized men and women in the name of the Lord Jesus, and they later received the Holy Spirit when Peter and John prayed for them (see 8:12-27). In Paul's conversion, Ananias prayed for his healing and for him to receive the Holy Spirit, and he was immediately baptized (see 9:17-18). Likewise, when the Holy Spirit comes upon the crowd of Gentile people here at Cornelius's house, Peter orders that they all be baptized, and then Cornelius and his guests invite him to stay for a few days (see 10:47-48; 11:14-17). As we shall see, this would prove to be a controversial decision.

BAPTISM IN THE EARLY CHURCH

Baptism in water was clearly an important practice in the early Jesus movement, but what is less clear is exactly *how* the practice was done. John's baptisms (like those performed for converts to the Jewish faith) were likely by immersion because they were performed in the Jordan River, but Luke does not tell us where the baptisms occurred in the book of Acts. In the story of Philip and the Ethiopian eunuch, for instance, Luke writes that they came to "some water" as they traveled along the road (8:36), but he does not elaborate on how much water was present or how Philip performed the baptism. We do know from archaeological and pictorial evidence that from the third century on a typical form of baptism was for a person to stand in water while it was poured over his or her body, but it is not certain if this was the practice employed in Acts.

We're also not told exactly *when* a person should be baptized. In Acts, the people being baptized are often adults making an adult confession, but at other times it's clear that some are infants or children who come under the head of a household.[2] In fact, as the narrative in Acts progresses, this becomes a more established pattern: the head of the household believes, and the entire household is baptized soon after. We see this not only in the story of Cornelius but also Lydia of Thyatira (see 16:14-15), the Philippian jailer (see 16:29-33), and Crispus, the synagogue leader in Corinth (see 18:8).

Based on this evidence, we can conclude that while we are not sure of the exact method or timing of baptism, it represents a form of Christian initiation that involves both water and "fire" (the infilling of the Holy Spirit), and that typically (but not always) these two things happen fairly close to each other.[3] The essential takeaways for us to keep in mind are that (1) the baptism God is most interested in is the baptism of the Holy Spirit, (2) that a person can receive the Holy Spirit anytime, even before his or her baptism, (3) that the external washing of water is symbolic of a person's sins being washed away by Jesus' death on the cross (see Acts 22:16; Titus 3:5), and (4) that believers in Jesus need to be incorporated into a group of believers. Baptism in water and baptism in the Holy Spirit are part of that incorporation.

REACTION FROM THE JERUSALEM CHURCH

Word of Peter's actions soon get back to the apostles in Jerusalem, and some of the Jewish believers hotly criticize him (see 11:1-3). How dare he treat the Gentiles as equals in the Holy Spirit?! It seems that Peter had a lot of 'splaining to do.

When Peter arrives back in Jerusalem, he goes over the story with the elders, repeating the episode of the strange sheet vision in almost exactly the same words (see verse 15). He reminds the elders that "the Lord" (Jesus) had said that John baptized with water but that they would be baptized in the Holy Spirit. Then he gave the kicker: If God wanted to give the gift of the Holy Spirit to the Gentiles, who were they (Jewish believers in Jesus) to stand in the way (see verse 17)?

With that, we read one of the most beautiful change of hearts recorded in Scripture: "When [the apostolic leaders in Jerusalem] heard this, they had no further objections and praised God, saying, 'So then, even to Gentiles God has granted repentance that leads to life'" (verse 18).

The First Jewish-Gentile Church

In Acts 11:19-30, Luke begins narrating the story of the first mixed Jewish-Gentile church. This body had been founded by Jewish believers in Jesus who had been scattered during the persecution that began with Stephen (see Acts 8). They had come to Antioch to preach the gospel to both Jews and Greeks. As a result, "a great number of people believed and turned to the Lord" (verse 21).

The apostolic leaders in Jerusalem hear about this unusual new church and send Barnabas to check things out. When Barnabas arrives, he likes what he sees and encourages them to remain true to Christ, and another wave of new believers come to the Lord (see verse 24). Barnabas then journeys to Tarsus, gets Saul-who-would-be-Paul, and together they instruct the new believers for a whole year. It is in Antioch where those who believe in Jesus are first called "Christians" (see verse 26).

In Acts 11:27, Luke tells us that there are some prophetic individuals in the Jerusalem church. One of them, Agabus, predicts through the Holy Spirit that a severe famine will hit Roman domains—a prediction that occurs in AD 43-44 during the reign of Emperor Claudius. In another beautiful tribute to the power of the gospel to change hearts, the mixed Jewish-Gentile church provides financial assistance during the famine to the home churches in Judea, and Barnabas and Paul bring the gift. When they later return to Antioch, they bring along Barnabas's cousin John Mark (see Acts 12:25).

Martyrdom and Miraculous Escapes

It is at this point that another wave of persecution breaks out. This time, King Herod Antipas (who had previously had John the Baptist beheaded) arrests members of the Jerusalem church, including the disciple James. He and his brother, John—whom Christ called "sons of thunder" (see Mark 3:17)—had been among the first disciples to join the Jesus movement (see Matthew 4:21-22).[4] James, Peter and John had been a part of Jesus' "inner circle," often accompanying Christ when other members of the Twelve were not included (see Matthew 17:1-9; Mark 5:37-42; Mark 14:32-36).

PETER'S ARREST AND ESCAPE

King Herod proceeds to have James executed by the sword, making him the first of the Twelve to be martyred for his faith (see Acts 12:1-2). The action meets with approval in the Jewish community, so Herod—ever the people-pleaser—arrests Peter as well. He places Peter in prison with the intention of holding a public trial after Passover. For all intents and purposes, Peter's fate is sealed.

But God has other plans. He sends an angel to the prison, who literally has to smack Peter to wake him up so he can escape. Peter follows the angel in a daze; he fully believes he is seeing another vision. It is not until the angel leads Peter past two guards and out of the gates of the city that he realizes what is actually taking place. Once he does, he says, "Now I know without a doubt that the Lord has sent his angel and rescued me from Herod's clutches and from everything the Jewish people were hoping would happen" (verse 11).

Peter goes to the home of Mary, the mother of John Mark, where a group of believers have gathered and are praying. Mary is apparently a woman of means, for the household has a servant named Rhoda, who answers the door. She is so excited when she hears Peter's voice that she runs to tell the others, leaving Peter out in the cold. The believers think she is crazy—they say it must be his "angel"—but Peter's continual knocking on the door ultimately convinces them to check out Rhoda's story.

When the Jewish believers open the door and see Peter standing there, they are once again "astonished." Peter settles them down and explains what transpired. Then he instructs them to "tell James and the other brothers and sisters about this" (verse 17). The "James" to whom Peter is referring here is James the brother of Jesus, who by this time was a prominent leader in the Jerusalem church (see Galatians 1:19; 2:9). A few years later, he will play an important role in presiding over the Jerusalem Council as the chief spokesman of the Church (see Acts 15:13-21).

THE DEATH OF HEROD AGRIPPA

After Passover that year, Herod travels to Caesarea to attend games performed in honor of Emperor Claudius. According to Josephus, when Herod entered the theater clad in his royal garments, the people cried,

"We have in the past honored you as a man, but now we honor you as one with a nature greater than any mortal being."[5] According to Luke, immediately afterward an angel of the Lord struck down Herod because he did not give praise to God, and he was "eaten by worms and died" (Acts 12:23). This is possibly a condition known as Fournier's gangrene, the same disease that might have killed his grandfather Herod the Great. Following this, Luke states that "the word of God continued to spread and flourish" (Acts 12:24).

Checks and Balances in Prophecy

It was the prophecies in Acts 9–10 that changed the mindset of the early Jewish believers and enabled the gospel to break out into the Gentile world. Prophecy was an important way the Holy Spirit moved people in the early Jesus movement to act. However, many Christians today do not understand how prophecy works, and as a result they are skeptical or frightened of it. There are many false prophets in the world who make predictions that simply do not come true (see session 6).

If we examine how Luke describes the prophecies in Acts 9–10, we see that there are a number of checks and balances in place—checks and balances that can help us discern when something is from the Holy Spirit and when it is not. First and foremost, those who received the prophecies in Acts were people of integrity who wanted to honor God in everything they did. No charlatans allowed! These individuals were attentive to the Holy Spirit and spent time with other believers and time alone with God. We see this especially in the example of Peter on the rooftop in Acts 10.

God often gave multiple words of prophecy to different people, and those words coincided with one another. For example, in Acts 9, while Jesus was meeting Saul on the road to Damascus, He was also giving a message to Ananias in the city. It didn't all depend on one approved person who was the only one allowed to hear God. God spoke to different servants and used the "little people" like Ananias, not just the head honchos.

Each of the prophecies was timed exquisitely. In Acts 10, God spoke to Cornelius and directed him to the home of Simon the tanner before He revealed the vision of the sheet from heaven to Peter. The men were downstairs and waiting for Peter by the time the Lord had finished revealing the prophecy to him. As believers, we have to believe that God can work providentially through these kinds of "coincidences."

The prophecies in Acts pointed to a discernable, God-glorifying purpose. They ultimately lifted up the name of Jesus. In addition, there weren't any formulas. The Holy Spirit was allowed to be creative and work through the spiritual senses that God had given His servants.

Whether it's through an inner voice, visions, trances, dreams or other ways, there's no single way that God communicates to us. We need to be open to the reality that God communicates to all kinds of people in all kinds of life situations—before they even believe in Jesus! Cornelius is a perfect case in point. The lesson here is that the Holy Spirit is always at work.

QUESTIONS FOR PERSONAL APPLICATION AND DISCUSSION

What was Peter's role in the Early Church? What miracles did the Lord perform through him in Lydda and Joppa?

_____

_____

_____

What is significant about Peter staying in the home of Simon the tanner? What is significant about him sharing a meal with Cornelius's messengers?

_____

_____

_____

_____

What was the vision that Peter received on the rooftop in Acts 10:9-23? What was the interpretation?

_____

_____

_____

Why is it significant that Luke mentions this vision six times in the book of Acts?

_____

_____

_____

_____

What happened to the Gentile believers in Joppa that astonished the Jewish believers? Why did this land Peter in some trouble back in Jerusalem?

_____

_____

_____

_____

In Galatians 1–2, Paul gives his own commentary on the events that took place during this time. Read Galatians 2:11-21. What issue does Paul raise in this passage? How does this relate to the events we read about Peter in Acts 9–11?

_____

_____

_____

_____

In Galatians 2:12, Paul mentions that Peter was afraid of "the circumcision group." These are believers in Jesus who taught that a Gentile who wanted to be a real follower of Jesus had to become Jewish and follow Mosaic Law. What might their argument have been?

_____

_____

_____

As Christians, it's easy for us to fall prey to religious thinking that says, if I'm doing good, God must like me more; or, if I'm doing bad, God must like me less. Why does Paul completely reject this mindset?

_____

_____

_____

_____

In Galatians 2:11-16, Paul was confrontational with Peter. Why do you think Paul was so direct? What was at stake?

_____

_____

_____

_____

In Acts 12, Peter has a miraculous escape from prison and goes to the home of Mary, where some believers have gathered. Why are they so astonished when Peter shows up at the door? What does Peter instruct them to do?

_____

_____

_____

_____

Many people today are skeptical or fearful of prophecy. What are some of the "checks and balances" given in Acts 9–10 for discerning a true word from God?

_____

_____

_____

_____

Do you believe that God speaks to believers today? If so, how does He communicate to us?

_____

_____

_____

_____

Notes

1. The effect of John's teaching on baptism was so widespread that it was still being administered 30 years later in Alexandria and Ephesus (see Acts 18:25; 19:1-7).
2. The Greek word for "household" (*oikos*) is a flexible term that included a person's immediate extended family (parents, uncles, aunts and cousins), any slaves and their families in service to that person, and any hired help.
3. This is the essential conclusion of scholars Killian McDonnell and George Montague in their book *Christian Initiation and Baptism in the Holy Spirit: Evidence from the First Eight Centuries* (Collegeville, MN: Liturgical Press, 1990.)
4. Some scholars have speculated that it might have been James's fiery temper that landed him in trouble with Herod. Jesus once rebuked him and his brother for asking if they could send fire down from heaven to destroy a Samaritan village (see Luke 9:51-56).
5. Flavius Josephus, *Antiquities of the Jews* (c. AD 94), 19:343-350.

Sources

Henrietta C. Mears, *What the Bible Is All About*, "Understanding Acts" (Ventura, CA: Regal Books, 2011), chapter 31.
Mears, *Highlights of Scripture, Part Four: Words and Works of Jesus, Teacher's Book* (Los Angeles, CA: The Gospel Light Press, 1937).

THAT GENEROUS DECISION
Free from the Law of Moses (Acts 13–15)

SESSION FOCUS

The spread of the gospel among the Gentiles in Antioch and other regions sparks a controversy within the early Jesus movement.

KEY VERSE TO MEMORIZE

This mystery is that through the gospel the Gentiles are heirs together with Israel, members together of one body, and sharers together in the promise in Christ Jesus.
EPHESIANS 3:6

WEEKLY READING

DAY 1	Ephesians 2
DAY 2	Galatians 3
DAY 3	Acts 13
DAY 4	Acts 14
DAY 5	Acts 15

FOR LEADERS: SESSION AT A GLANCE

SESSION OUTLINE	60 MIN.	90 MIN.	WHAT YOU WILL DO
Getting started	10	15	Pray and worship
Main points of the chapter	25	35	Discuss how Jesus is God's Word to us
Application and discussion	15	25	Discuss the generous decision the Jewish church made in regard to the Gentiles and its implications for us
Looking ahead	5	5	Prepare for next week
Wrapping up	5	10	Close with prayer or song

A Situation in Flux

King Herod Agrippa died in AD 44, so by this point only 11 or 12 years have passed since the crucifixion and resurrection of Jesus. We are still early in the story of the Jesus movement, and the Church in Acts is on a steep learning curve. Monumental changes are happening fast that require monumental decisions to be made. Another round of persecution could break out suddenly at any time. It's a situation in flux.

In the midst of these changes, the mother church in Jerusalem continues to closely monitor everything that is taking place. The apostles have their eyes open and their ears to the ground. They're watching and listening for what the Holy Spirit is doing among the Gentile communities, but they are also wary of potential pitfalls. In some cases, a respected leader in the Jerusalem church (such as Peter, John and Barnabas) makes a decision, but at other times a recognized leader (such as Philip) makes a call on the fly.

Regardless, none of the leaders in the Jerusalem church put the brakes on the movement or tried to slow it down. They are cautious, but when they see the Holy Spirit move in a situation, they go with it. They don't let tradition, procedures or manmade rules get in the way.

THE ANTIOCHEAN EXPERIMENT

When we last left Paul and Barnabas in Acts 11, they were working together in Antioch in the first Jewish-Gentile church. It was a grand experiment, the crucible by which Paul worked out his understanding of the one "new humanity" and the one "Body of Christ." In this new unified body of believers, reconciliation between God and people reigned, the walls between Jews and Gentiles were brought down, diversity of backgrounds and spiritual gifts were accepted, and being of one mind for the purposes of glorifying Jesus Christ in the world was celebrated.

In Ephesians 2, Paul lays the groundwork for these ideas. He states that because of God's magnificent grace, believers in Christ have been made alive and made new in Him (see verses 4-7). As a result, they are to live out this truth and be reconciled to one another (see verses 11-22). In Galatians 3, Paul extends this principle of unity in Christ to breaking down human barriers between people: "There is neither Jew nor Gentile, neither slave nor free, nor is there male and female, for you are all one in Christ Jesus" (verse 28). The believers in Antioch took these principles to heart, and they became the core values that drove them to reach out in love with the gospel to their world.

FIRST FORAY INTO FOREIGN MISSIONS

Technically, we could say that Christian missions first began with the mother church in Jerusalem. After all, that was where Jesus' 11 remaining disciples (and Matthias, who was chosen to replace Judas) had their base of operations, and that was where the Holy Spirit was first poured out on the Day of Pentecost. It was also from Jerusalem that Philip, Peter, Barnabas and others first reached out with the gospel to the nearby foreign lands of Judea, Samaria, Galilee, Ethiopia and Syria.

However, the Jerusalem church was just a tad too committed to Mosaic law to easily embrace the idea of cross-cultural missions to the Gentiles. On the other hand, the Antiochean church oozed cultural diversity. In Acts 13:1, Luke tells us, "In the church at Antioch there were prophets and teachers: Barnabas, Simeon called Niger, Lucius of Cyrene, Manaen (who had been brought up with Herod the tetrarch) and Saul." Barnabas and Paul had a Hebraic Jewish background. Simeon, called Niger, might have been a black African. Lucius was a Greek, and Manaen had grown up in the heights of high society. Yet as diverse as they were, they were united in glorifying Jesus.

It was not the people in Antioch who initiated this cross-cultural mission, but rather the Holy Spirit. The church didn't rush this effort, and it didn't happen right away. In fact, Paul and Barnabas poured out their hearts and lives for a whole year in that town. Before anybody was sent anywhere, they waited until the Holy Spirit spoke.

Worshiping the Lord and fasting were normal for both the Jerusalem church and the church in Antioch, and the Holy Spirit had gifted each with prophets and teachers. On this occasion, the Holy Spirit speaks to these individuals at Antioch and says, "Set apart for me Barnabas and Saul for the work to which I have called them" (13:2). So the leaders pray, fast, lay their hands on Barnabas and Paul in dedication and commissioning, and send them on their way.

TO THE JEWS FIRST

After the leaders in Antioch send off Paul and Barnabas, the two men travel to the port city of Seleucia and set sail for the island of Cyprus (see map on pages 160-161). Once there, they are joined by John Mark from the Jerusalem church and begin to proclaim the word of God in the Jewish synagogues. This is significant, for even though Paul and Barnabas had a direct commission from Christ to go to the Gentiles, they never forgot their own people. Wherever they went, they first preached in synagogues on the Sabbath days, hoping to give the Jewish people the first chance at responding to the gospel (see Acts 13:5; 13:14-15,42,44; 14:1; 17:2; 18:4; Romans 1:16). This was only right, as the promises of God about Jesus as Messiah came from the Hebrew Bible, and the Hebrew people had preserved those promises in the Scriptures.

Yet there was another reason Paul and the other apostles employed this strategy. Jewish synagogues were spread all over the Eastern Mediterranean, and many of these synagogues had attracted non-Jews (such as Cornelius in Acts 10) to their worship services. These people of pagan backgrounds ("God-fearers") were tired of their old religions and intrigued by the Jews' belief in one true God. By preaching in synagogues, Paul, Barnabas and John could reach out to mixed audiences of Jews and God-fearers, at least some of whom the Holy Spirit had prepared to accept Jesus as Messiah (see Acts 13:13-48 for a good example of this). It was an act of love on their part, and it was also good missions strategy.

Undoubtedly this was not Paul and his companions' only strategy in reaching the Gentile populations with the gospel. In 1 Thessalonians 2:9, Paul writes, "Surely you remember, brothers and sisters, our toil and hardship; we worked night and day in order not to be a burden to anyone while we preached the gospel of God to you." This has led some scholars to conclude that Paul was actually *working*—supporting himself so as not to be a burden on the community—while he was sharing the gospel.

In Acts 18:3, Luke states that Paul was a tentmaker by trade, so one scenario would be that when Paul and his companions came to a new town, they obtained a space near the city center and set up a shop. As people stopped by to do business, Paul and the others would take the opportunity to share the message of Christ with them. This would not be an unusual practice, for in the ancient world people typically used shops for passing along news, reports and rumors and for engaging in small talk. As the customers were drawn in by the message, they frequented the shop to learn more, until small weekly gatherings were established. These converts would then share the gospel with their households, and the message would spread.

MISUNDERSTANDING AND OPPOSITION
Luke tells us that the reactions to the apostles' teaching were mixed. In Pisidian Antioch, some of the people hear the message gladly and believe (see Acts 13:42-49), but the Jewish leaders incite others in high society (some of

them God-fearers) to expel Paul and Barnabas from their city (see 13:49-52). In Iconium, a more sinister plot to mistreat and stone Paul and Barnabas is uncovered, and they are able to escape (see 14:2-6). In Lystra, after a notable miracle is performed, the people claim, "The gods have come down to us in human form!" and want to worship Paul and Barnabas (see 14:8-18). There, some of Paul's enemies from Antioch and Iconium finally catch up with him and stone him, leaving him for dead (see 14:19-20). Paul survives, but he must have been extremely sore for a good while. Missions was a grand experiment for the church in Antioch—certainly one not for the faint of heart—and it continues to be a grand experiment today.

A COOPERATIVE VENTURE

After Paul's close brush with death in Lystra, he and his companions travel to Derbe and then return to Pisidian Antioch, encouraging the believers in each place and appointing elders for the new churches. They travel to Pamphylia, Perga and the coastal city of Attalia, and then finally return to the church in Antioch. There they report all that God had done and how the Holy Spirit had enabled them to reach the Gentiles.

Paul and Barnabas's first missionary journey had been a success, and it had come about as a result of a unique partnership between the church in Antioch, the mother church in Jerusalem, and the Holy Spirit. For the first time, new Gentile churches had been established in the provinces in Asia Minor (modern-day Turkey). However, with these new converts came new controversy, for the church in Jerusalem now had to decide whether to impose Jewish traditions upon these Gentile believers.

A Controversy Erupts

In Acts 15, the mother church in Jerusalem is faced with a difficult controversy. The flashpoint is circumcision—an issue that was symbolic of a number of other concerns that had been brewing as to how far Gentile believers had to go in adopting Jewish practices. The time had come to determine the relationship between Jewish identity and the new Jesus movement and the relationship of the gospel to the Mosaic Law. In making this critical decision—one that would change the direction of the movement from a sect within Judaism to a worldwide faith—the leaders of the Jerusalem church would once again rely on the guidance of the Holy Spirit (see Acts 15:28).

THE SPARK

The spark that lights the fireworks occurs when a group of people come down from Judea to the Antioch church and begin teaching that unless the Gentile believers are circumcised "according to the custom taught by Moses," they cannot be saved (Acts 15:1). This is a direct challenge to the gospel as preached by Paul and Barnabas, and they reacted strongly to what these individuals were saying. Ultimately, the church in Antioch appoints Paul, Barnabas and a few others to go to Jerusalem to discuss the matter with the apostles and elders.

As it turns out, the group who brought the teaching to Antioch includes Pharisees who had come to believe in Jesus. At this time, there were Jewish proselytizers who sought to convert Gentiles to Judaism. Jesus spoke about them negatively in Matthew 23:15, saying, "Woe to you, teachers of the law and Pharisees, you hypocrites! You travel over land and sea to win a single convert, and when you have succeeded, you make them twice as much a child of hell as you are." When these proselytizers made Gentile converts, those converts were not considered "fully Jewish" until the men in the group had undergone circumcision.

THE AGENDA

Circumcision was thus the gateway into Judaism and into fulfilling all of the Mosaic laws. In this way, the former Pharisees were attempting to get the Jerusalem church to conform to their model for converting Gentiles. They were concerned that the Church was getting ready to throw out Mosaic Law, and they wanted to make their position known. In addition, it is possible that nationalist pressure was increasing in Judea and these believers wanted to make a statement that they were not being disloyal to their Jewish heritage.

There were three major problems with these former Pharisees' approach. First, their method ignored (and even negated) what the Holy Spirit had been doing for at least a decade in breaking down the walls of separation between the Jews and the Gentiles. Second, it fatally compromised the principle of salvation by grace through faith—Jesus had come to the world to purchase salvation on the cross for the very reason that people could not save themselves by means of the Mosaic Law. Third, it communicated to the Gentiles that they weren't genuine believers in Jesus unless they were willing to get circumcised and follow all the other laws of Moses.

The Great Debate

The apostles and elders in Jerusalem hear both sides and then meet together to consider the question. The first to speak at the council is Peter. He begins by reminding the assembly of his experience with Cornelius in Acts 10, stating that God had made a choice that the Gentiles would hear the message of the gospel from him (see Acts 15:7). Peter goes on to state that God already accepted the Gentiles who believed in Jesus because He had given them the Holy Spirit, *just as God had given the Holy Spirit to the Jewish believers on the Day of Pentecost* (see verse 8).

Peter's third point to the council is that God does not play favorites between Jews and Gentiles because He purifies people's hearts through faith, *not by conformity to the laws of Moses* (see verse 9). Finally, he argues that it would be testing God—and would make no sense—to place on the necks of the Gentiles "a yoke that neither we nor our fathers have been able to bear," referring to the yoke of all the 613 Mosaic laws and their interpretations as they grew with Jewish tradition (verse 10).

JAMES, THE ELDER STATESMAN

After Peter's address, Paul and Barnabas get up and tell about how God had confirmed the preaching of the word with miraculous signs (see verse 12). Finally, James speaks up. As previously mentioned, this James is the brother of Jesus, and as the elder statesman of the church in Jerusalem, he is allowed to have the last word on the matter. What he says will carry a lot of weight.

James begins by summarizing the main points made in the meeting (the consensus, if there is one). He says that Simeon (the Hebrew way of saying the name Simon, whom we know as Peter) described how God began the project of making a people for Himself from the Gentiles. James proceeds to show how this was foretold in Scripture, quoting Amos's prophecy of "David's fallen tent," a passage of Scripture that would have been well known to the Jews

In this prophecy, Amos, writing some 200 years after King Solomon died and the Davidic kingdom had split into two kingdoms, gives this oracle from the Lord: "After this I will return and rebuild David's fallen tent. Its ruins I will rebuild, and I will restore it, that the rest of mankind may seek the Lord, even all the Gentiles who bear my name" (Acts 15:16-17; see Amos 9:11-12). Two of Jesus' Messianic titles were "Son of David" and "Son of God." In this way, Jesus was the new King of Israel who inherited all the promises God made to David about an everlasting kingdom (see 2 Samuel 7:14). James is thus showing that the winning of the Gentiles to Christ is an integral part of Amos's prophecy in restoring this "fallen tent."

A GENEROUS DECISION

After stating the prophecy from Amos, James—himself a Hebraic Jewish believer in Jesus—concludes in favor of the innovative, Spirit-led cross-cultural missionizing of Peter, Paul and Barnabas. He says, "It is my judgment, therefore, that we should not make it difficult for the Gentiles who are turning to God. Instead we should write to them, telling them to abstain from food polluted by idols, from sexual immorality, from the meat of strangled animals and from blood" (15:19-20). James also affirms that the decision has been given by the Holy Spirit and that the Jerusalem Council has listened corporately to the Spirit in making this decision: "It seemed good to the Holy Spirit and to us not to burden you with anything beyond the following requirements" (verse 28).

This was an amazingly generous decision. From this point on, Gentile believers would no longer be subject to all the rigors of Mosaic Law. However, James does stress three basic items that all believers in Christ should avoid: (1) food sacrificed to idols (meat offered in sacrifice to idols and then eaten in a temple feast or sold in a shop), (2) blood and the meat of strangled animals (a method of slaughter in which the blood remained in the meat), and (3) sexual immorality. These regulations, which appear to be based on the laws given in Leviticus 18:6-18, would have given particular offense to more traditional Jews, and they were also quite prevalent in the cultures in which the new Gentile converts found themselves.

THE REGULATIONS

Regarding the first item, almost *all* meat in Greek and Roman societies was offered to pagan gods before being made available in the meat stalls in the market, so most of the meat was tainted with idolatry. Perhaps for this reason, Paul would later modify this item in Romans 14 and 1 Corinthians 11 to allow for differences of opinion on the matter as long as people were acting in faith and not deliberately acting in ways that would cause others to stumble. As he states to the Roman believers, "If your brother or sister is distressed because of what you eat, you are no longer acting in love. Do not by your eating destroy someone for whom Christ died" (Romans 14:15).

For the second item, as previously mentioned, rules regarding sexuality were relaxed in pagan societies (at least for men), while sexual morality for both sexes was important in the Jewish community. Sexual morality was also important in the emerging Jesus movement because it was a central plank in Jesus' message on human dignity (see Matthew 5:27-30). For this reason, this second caution should not have caused surprise or objection from anyone in the Christian community.

The third items to avoid were meat that came from strangled animals and blood. The Jews were particular about blood because God had been particular about blood in His covenant with the Israelites. In Mosaic Law, a person was not to eat the blood of animals (see Genesis 9:4) because "life" was seen to be in the blood of a creature and blood was used to atone for the sins of people (see Leviticus 17:10-14; Deuteronomy 12:23). Even foreigners who lived among the Israelites had to abide by this law. There was also a principle that animals had to be killed humanely and their blood completely drained from their carcasses. Strangling an animal was a horrible way for it to die—it was not humane and didn't allow for the complete draining of blood.

A Letter to the Churches

After making this ruling, James and the rest of the council draft a letter to the Gentile churches in Antioch, Syria and Cilicia, telling them not to be disturbed by those who were trying to put Gentiles under Mosaic Law. In the letter, the council states that these individuals did not represent the Jerusalem church and that they were not authorized by them to proclaim their misguided teachings (see Acts 15:22-33). The council also notes that two elders in the Jerusalem church are delivering the letter: Judas (called Barsabbas) and Silas. Judas is not again mentioned, but Silas will become a traveling companion of Paul and an important figure in the Church (see Acts 15:40; 1 Thessalonians 1:1; 2 Corinthians 1:19; 1 Peter 5:12).

The Effects of the Decision

As a result of this decision, the gospel could spread like wildfire among the Gentiles. There was no longer any question about whether the churches should put Gentiles under Jewish law. The ethical standards in the Church were now specified as being about faith, freedom of conscience (under clear moral principles found in the Ten Commandments), obeying the spirit as opposed to the letter of the law, and being attentive to the motions of the Holy Spirit in bringing goodness to others.

This is exactly what happened. Despite persecution, false teachers and deliberate attempts to compromise the message of Jesus with other religious viewpoints, the gospel spread to Gentile communities throughout the known world. By the fourth century AD, there were so many Christians in the Roman Empire that it became a matter of political prudence—if not personal faith alone—for the emperor Constantine to legalize Christianity and then make it the official religion of the empire.

QUESTIONS FOR PERSONAL APPLICATION AND DISCUSSION

In Acts 6:2, Luke states that the apostles in Jerusalem prioritized "the ministry of the word of God" over waiting on tables, which apparently some of them had been doing. Read Matthew 20:25-28 and John 13:1-17. Why were the Twelve performing such acts of service? In making evangelism a priority, was the Jerusalem church stating that these tasks were unimportant? Why or why not?

_____

_____

_____

_____

The Jerusalem church encouraged the spread of the gospel but was wary of potential pitfalls. For each event below, list the action taken by the apostles.

EVENT	ACTION TAKEN
The Samaritans accept the word of God (see Acts 8:14-17).	
An Ethiopian eunuch receives the word of God and desires to be baptized (Acts 8:36-38).	
Saul, persecutor of the Early Church, becomes a believer and travels to meet with the disciples in Jerusalem (Acts 9:1-30).	

EVENT	ACTION TAKEN
The Gentiles in Cornelius's household receive the Holy Spirit (Acts 10:23-48).	
The Jewish believers in Jerusalem learn that Peter has gone into a Gentile's house and eaten with him (Acts 11:1-18).	
News reaches the Jerusalem church that Jewish evangelists have led many Gentiles in Antioch to faith in Jesus (see Acts 11:19-26).	

How did Paul, Barnabas and other church leaders spread the gospel when they reached a new town? In what ways was this effective in reaching both Jewish and Gentile communities?

_____

_____

_____

Acts 13–14 reads much like a travelogue of Paul and Barnabas's first missionary journey. For each passage listed below, write the place the apostles visited and the general reaction they received to the message of Christ.

PASSAGE	PLACE	RESPONSE
Acts 13:4-12		
Acts 13:13-50		
Acts 13:51–14:7		
Acts 14:8-19		
Acts 14:20-21		

Paul and Barnabas were two of the Early Church's best communicators, and yet they were often met with misunderstanding, opposition and even persecution. What lesson can we take from this when we are attempting to bring the gospel to others?

_____

_____

_____

What was the "spark" that ignited the controversy between Jewish and Gentile believers? In what ways had this debate been brewing for some time?

_____

_____

_____

What were the two positions represented at the Jerusalem Council? Which position was closer to what Jesus said and did (see Matthew 5:17)? Why?

_____

_____

_____

The Jerusalem Council effectively ruled that if you were a Jewish believer in Jesus and wanted to continue following the Mosaic Law, that was fine, but if you were a Gentile believer, you didn't have to follow all the Mosaic laws. What makes this decision so affirming, freeing and life-giving?

_____

_____

_____

What was the short-term effect of the council's decision? What was the long-term effect?

_____

_____

_____

Sources

I. Howard Marshall, *The Acts of the Apostles: An Introduction and Commentary*, Tyndale New Testament Commentaries (Grand Rapids, MI: William B. Eerdmans, 1989), p. 126.

Henrietta C. Mears, *What the Bible Is All About*, "Understanding Acts" (Ventura, CA: Regal Books, 2011), chapter 31.

Mears, *Highlights of Scripture, Part Four: Words and Works of Jesus, Teacher's Book* (Los Angeles, CA: The Gospel Light Press, 1937).

COME SAIL AWAY

Paul's Missionary Work Among the Gentiles (Acts 16–21:16)

SESSION FOCUS

The decision of the Jerusalem Council opens the door for the gospel to be preached to the Gentiles in the known world.

KEY VERSES TO MEMORIZE

I have not hesitated to preach anything that would be helpful to you but have taught you publicly and from house to house. I have declared to both Jews and Greeks that they must turn to God in repentance and have faith in our Lord Jesus.
ACTS 20:20-21

WEEKLY READING

DAY 1	Acts 16
DAY 2	Acts 17
DAY 3	Acts 18
DAY 4	Acts 19-20
DAY 5	Acts 21:1-16

FOR LEADERS: SESSION AT A GLANCE

SESSION OUTLINE	60 MIN.	90 MIN.	WHAT YOU WILL DO
Getting started	10	15	Pray and worship
Main points of the chapter	25	35	Discuss how Jesus is God's Word to us
Application and discussion	15	25	Discuss Paul's missions strategy and how he planted churches throughout the known world
Looking ahead	5	5	Prepare for next week
Wrapping up	5	10	Close with prayer or song

Applying the Council's Decision

After the decision of the Jerusalem Council is disseminated (see Acts 15:26), Paul and Barnabas have a sharp disagreement about whether to take Mark (also known as John Mark), who had deserted the missionary band in Pamphylia, on the next journey. Paul thinks Mark is untrustworthy, but Barnabas wants to give him another chance (see 15:36-40). So they split. Paul takes Silas with him and moves into Asia Minor (Syria and Cilicia), while Barnabas takes Mark with him to Cyprus.

There is a significant point here that is often overlooked: Luke makes no mention that either Paul or Barnabas fasted or sought the Holy Spirit's guidance in making this decision. If they had, this conflict might never have occurred. As it turns out, Barnabas made the right call on this one: Mark serves Barnabas with distinction, and later Paul and Mark reconcile. In a tender moment near the end of Paul's life, the apostle even makes a special request for Mark to come to him because he "is helpful in my ministry" (2 Timothy 4:11).

PAUL AND THE MOSAIC LAW

The next several chapters in Acts cover Paul's second missionary journey (16:1–18:22) and his third missionary journey (18:23–21:18). In the second journey, Paul and Silas travel to Lystra, where they pick up a missionary colleague named Timothy (see map on pages 160-161). Timothy represents in his own person the mixed Jewish-Gentile churches: his mother is Jewish, and his father is Greek. Before they start the journey, Paul does something striking, puzzling and instructive.

In the book of Galatians, written shortly after the decision of the Jerusalem Council, Paul had said in no uncertain terms that Christ died to set people free from regulations of Mosaic Law. With the events still fresh in his mind, Paul speaks with passion to this group of believers: "You foolish Galatians! Who has bewitched you? . . . Did you receive the Spirit by the works of the law, or by believing what you heard? . . . Who cut in on you to keep you from obeying the truth? . . . I wish they [those who were promoting the needs for circumcision] would go the whole way and emasculate themselves!" (Galatians 3:1-2; 5:7,12).

Paul stresses to the Galatians that circumcision is of no value to them, for taking it on will only put them under obligation to follow the whole Mosaic Law. He writes, "The only thing that counts is faith expressing itself through love. . . . Neither circumcision nor uncircumcision means anything;

what counts is the new creation" (5:6; 6:15). And yet, in Acts 16:1-3, Paul has Timothy circumcised. What was Paul thinking? Was he saying one thing and doing another? Was he aware of this apparent inconsistency?

The only explanation that Luke gives in Acts is that Paul had this done because Timothy was from that area and the Jews there "all knew that [Timothy's] father was a Greek" (16:3). It is possible that part of Paul's motivation might have been to mollify the Jewish believers in the area. After all, they were likely still stinging from the decision of the Jerusalem Council, and Timothy's circumcision could be seen as a type of peace offering. However, Paul wasn't an extremely mollifying kind of guy. There is probably a better explanation.

PAUL'S GUIDING PRINCIPLE

The more likely explanation is that Paul had a missionary perspective. He wanted to use his freedom to advance the gospel and not hinder it unnecessarily (see 1 Corinthians 9:19-22). He took on the Jews' culture when he was among them, but was not slavishly devoted to it, and he took on the Greeks' culture when he was among them, provided it did not directly contradict the gospel or its values.

This missionary principle helps us understand not only why Paul had Timothy circumcised but also other actions that Paul takes throughout the book of Acts. For instance, in Acts 18:18 Paul takes a vow upon himself (probably a temporary Nazarite vow as described in Numbers 6), and then later sponsors some Jewish brothers on their own vow (see 21:20-26). He continues to celebrate Jewish festivals (see 20:6). In his letter to the Roman believers, he carefully words his teaching on showing deference to one another in regard to Jewish and pagan customs and leaves his conclusion open-ended (see Romans 14:22-23).

For Gentiles, Paul's teaching was a departure from anything they had known, but for people with Jewish backgrounds, it was especially radical. In his letter to the Colossian believers, Paul writes, "Therefore do not let anyone judge you by what you eat or drink, or with regard to a religious festival, a New Moon celebration or a Sabbath day" (Colossians 2:16). God had commanded these religious festivals, New Moon festivals and the Sabbath day in the Old Testament. The Sabbath, in particular, had been called "lasting covenant" for generations to come (see Exodus 31:16). Yet something about Jesus' coming had radically altered how the people were to understand the Mosaic laws. Paul's teaching was strong medicine, but it had the ultimate purpose of promoting peace, reconciliation and the advancement of the gospel.

Sometimes Paul's strategy worked, and sometimes it didn't. The accusation that Paul was out to destroy Jewish law and customs dogged him wherever he went, and it even played a role in the events leading up to his arrest. This is why, as we will see, he frequently gets into trouble with Jewish traditionalists. But, like Jesus, Paul wasn't out to destroy the law. At the deepest level, he wanted to fulfill it (see Matthew 5:17; Romans 13:8,10; Galatians 5:14; 6:2).

The Gospel Goes to Greece

From Derbe and Lystra, Paul and his companions travel northeast through the province of Galatia. But when they reach the border, something unexpected happens: the Holy Spirit prevents them from preaching the word in the next province of Asia. Luke does not tell us what exactly this was—it was perhaps a prophetic word to the group—but it was significant enough to divert their travel plans. The same thing occurs when they try to enter Bithynia. So Paul and his companions head north and then east to the city of Alexandria Troas, located on the coast of the Aegean Sea (see Acts 16:6-8).

During the night, Paul has a vision of a man in Macedonia who begs him to come and help them. Unlike the earlier episode with John Mark, this time Paul heeds the voice of the Holy Spirit and makes plans to journey to the Greek island of Samothrace and on to Neopolis (modern-day Kavala), the port city for Philippi, located some 10 miles away (see Acts 16:9-12). Interestingly, in verse 10 Luke uses the pronoun "we" for the first time, which seems to indicate that he joined Paul and the others in Troas.[1]

TROUBLE IN PHILIPPI

Philippi (present-day Filippoi) was an ancient town that had been established by Philip of Macedon, the father of Alexander the Great, in 356 BC. Philip had founded the town because of its strategic location and to take control of the nearby gold mines. After the Roman generals Antony and Octavian (later known as Emperor Augustus) took the city in 42 BC, it became a settlement for veteran Roman soldiers.

As previously discussed, Paul's typical strategy when reaching a new city was to go to the synagogue and share the gospel there. Philippi did not have a synagogue, so the Jewish women in the area observed the Sabbath by meeting at "a place of prayer" outside the city near a river (Acts 16:13). One of the women there is Lydia, a God-fearing Gentile who had a business in trading cloth. She is likely cultured, well educated, widely traveled and wealthy. When she hears Paul's message, she becomes a believer in Christ, and she and her entire household are baptized (see verses 14-15).

One time when Paul and the others are visiting this place of prayer, a female slave who has "a spirit" by which she predicts the future encounters them. In the original Greek this is literally a "Python spirit" (Greek *pythona*), referring to a mystical serpent that was believed to have guarded the oracle at Delphi—an individual with a demonically empowered gift of prophecy.[2] The slave woman was apparently quite accurate, as she made a lot of money for her owners.

Similar to other stories of demon possession that we find in Luke's Gospel (see 4:34,41; 8:28), the spirit in this woman proclaims knowledge about what Paul and the others were doing in Philippi, stating, "These men are servants of the Most High God, who are telling you the way to be saved" (Acts 16:17). She keeps this up for so long that eventually Paul becomes annoyed and commands the spirit to leave her. As might be expected, this does not sit well with her owners, who have now lost their means of making money. So they round up Paul and Silas, take them before the authorities, and accuse them of advocating "customs unlawful for us as Romans to accept or practice" (verse 21). When the crowd joins in, the authorities decide to take action.

Paul and Silas are beaten with rods, taken to prison, and placed in the innermost cells with their feet in stocks. The pain and discomfort from the beatings keep them awake, but instead of giving in to despair and questioning why this has occurred, the two begin praying and singing hymns. Unlike Peter's jailbreak in Acts 12, this time God sends an earthquake that shakes *all* of the prisoners' chains loose. The jailer, who is apparently concerned the prisoners' escape will be blamed on his negligence (a capital offense), draws his sword to kill himself, but Paul tells him that all of the prisoners are still there. He and Silas share the gospel with the jailer, and he also comes to believe in Christ as the Messiah. As with Lydia, he and his household are immediately baptized, and in the morning the magistrates order the release of Paul and Silas (see verses 22-36).

Paul and Silas know that to leave the city in this way would set a dangerous precedent for their future treatment, so they send a message to the magistrates that they are Roman citizens, and that as such they should have been exempt from public beatings without a trial. The magistrates become alarmed and attempt to appease the two by escorting them personally out of the prison. Then they ask Paul and his companions to leave the city (see verses 37-40). Lydia and the jailer become the founders of the church in Philippi.

A RIOT IN THESSALONICA

From Philippi, Paul and his companions travel along the Via Egnatia, the great Roman highway, southwest to the cities of Amphipolis and Apollonia and then northwest to Thessalonica, the capital of Macedonia. King Cassander of Macedon had founded the city around 315 BC, naming it after his wife, Thessalonike, a half-sister of Alexander the Great. The Romans had made Thessalonica a "free city" in 42 BC, and it had a large enough Jewish population to have a synagogue.

Once again, Paul and his companions begin their ministry by sharing the gospel in the synagogue. Luke states that he reasons with the Jews there for three Sabbaths, although his stay there is probably longer, as Paul notes in 1 Thessalonians 2:9 that he worked among them during this stay and in Philippians 4:15-16 that he was there long enough to receive monetary gifts from the church in Philippi. Many of the Jews and God-fearing Greeks join Paul and Silas, as did "quite a few prominent women" (Acts 17:4), which could refer to women of the upper class or the wives of leaders in the city.

Once again, some traditionalist Jews stir up trouble. They incite a riot, and a mob rushes to the home of Jason, who was hosting the missionaries. The rioters can't locate Paul or Silas, so they drag Jason and other believers before the popular assembly (Greek *demos*) that governs the free city. They claim that Paul and Silas are teaching about a new king named Jesus, and thus are traitors against Caesar (the Roman Emperor Claudius Caesar, who began his reign in AD 41). Jason is able to post bond, and that night he and the other believers get Paul and Silas out of the city (see verses 5-9).

THE FAIR-MINDED BEREANS

The missionaries journey about 45 miles southwest to Berea (modern-day Verria), which the Roman statesman Cicero had described as an "out-of-the-way town," probably because it was off the main Roman highway (see Acts 17:10). The city had a synagogue, which is likely why Paul and his group chose to minister there. Unlike in Thessalonica, the Jews of Berea are of "noble character" (verse 11) because they check what Paul and Silas are saying against the Hebrew Scriptures. They are not only knowledgeable about God's Word but also open to the move of God's Holy Spirit, and many come to believe in Jesus as the Messiah. Unfortunately, the rabble-rousers from Thessalonica infiltrate the city and again stir up the crowds. The believers send Paul on alone to Athens, to later be joined there by Timothy and Silas (see verses 12-15).

BATTLING THE PHILOSOPHERS IN ATHENS

Athens is one of the world's oldest cities, with a history spanning some 3,400 years. It became a powerful city-state in 480 BC when a group of Greek cities (known as the Delian League) defeated the mighty Persian armies at Salamis. Even after the Romans conquered the city in 146 BC, Athens continued to be a center of learning and philosophy, though in a much reduced state. In Paul's day it was "full of idols" (Acts 16:16), and some historians have estimated that more images of Greek gods were located in Athens than in all the rest of Greece combined.

Paul again takes the message of the gospel to the Jews and God-fearing Greeks in the synagogue, and he also speaks in the marketplace (perhaps setting up a shop there). There he is met by two groups of philosophers: the Epicureans and the Stoics. The Epicureans, founded by Epicurus (341–270 BC), tended to believe that the gods did not exist or that they were removed from human affairs. The Stoics, founded by Zeno (340–265 BC), believed reason to be the guiding principle in the universe. They took Paul to the Areopagus (literally "Ares' Hill" or "Mars' Hill"), which was either a form of a ruling body that met on a hill that overlooked the city or just a gathering of philosophers (see verses 17-21).

The assembly gives Paul the opportunity to share the gospel. This time, he draws on his knowledge of Greek philosophers as well as his knowledge of Hebrew Scripture. He tells the Athenians of an altar he has seen bearing the inscription "TO AN UNKNOWN GOD" (verse 23), and uses this to introduce *the* one true God of the universe—a God whom they did not know. Paul continues to address the group, drawing from the Greeks' own secular sources and, through the guidance of the Holy Spirit, discerning God's truth in them.

When Paul mentions that Christ has risen from the dead, the group is divided. Some of them sneer at him, but others want to hear more. These individuals ultimately become followers of Christ (see verses 14-34).

No Harm in Corinth

After Paul's somewhat unsuccessful stop in Athens, he travels west to Corinth. Like Athens, Corinth had been a powerful city-state before the Romans virtually destroyed it in 146 BC. By Paul's time the city had been rebuilt, and it served as a center of trade and commerce, with a population of perhaps more than 200,000 that consisted of Romans, Greeks and Jews. Luke tells us that the Roman proconsul Gallio was ruling at the time (see Acts 18:12), so Paul would have arrived in Corinth in the fall of AD 50 and would have left in the spring of AD 52.

One of the first things Paul does in the city is meet up with a Jewish believer named Aquila and his wife, Priscilla, who had been forced to leave Rome after Emperor Claudius issued an edict in AD 49–50 expelling all Jews from the city. Paul stays in their home, works as a tentmaker and does his typical routine of reasoning with the Jews and God-fearers in the local synagogue. Silas and Timothy finally join Paul at this time, and the group devotes themselves to preaching to the residents of the city (see verses 2-5).

When the Jews oppose Paul and become abusive, he becomes frustrated with them and, similar to an earlier occasion in which he "shook the dust" off his feet (Acts 13:51), he breaks fellowship with them and states that he will "go to the Gentiles" (Acts 18:6). It was the Jews who typically performed this action against the Gentiles. By flipping it around, Luke indicates that these Jews who rejected the gospel were no better than the Gentiles who were cut off from the people of God. In spite of this, however, Paul keeps preaching to Jews, such as Crispus, the synagogue leader, who believes in Jesus along with his whole household (see verses 7-8).

One night, the Lord speaks to Paul in a vision and tells him that no one will harm him while he is in the city. This proves to be true when the Jews make an attack against him and bring him before Gallio. The proconsul refuses to get involved in the matter, as the charges did not fall under crimes against the state and he has no jurisdiction, and he tells the Jewish leaders to settle the matter themselves (see verses 9-16). After this, Paul stays in Corinth for some time and then, accompanied by Priscilla and Aquila, heads for Ephesus. The couple stays in Ephesus while Paul sails back to Caesarea, laying the groundwork for his return. From there Paul visits the mother church in Jerusalem and then returns to his home base in Antioch (see verses 19-23).

Return to the Gentile Churches

While Paul is on "furlough" in Jerusalem and Antioch, some events are taking place behind the scenes in Ephesus. A Jewish believer from Alexandra, Egypt (the second largest city in the Roman Empire), arrives and begins teaching about Jesus. This man is known as Apollos (shortened from Apollonius), and he will become a well-known figure in Christianity. But he has evidently picked up some erroneous ideas about Christian faith in Alexandria that need to be corrected, so Priscilla and Aquila took him into their home and explained the true gospel to him (see Acts 18:24-26).

When Paul arrives in Ephesus, he meets up with 12 men who are apparently disciples of Apollos (see Acts 19:1-2). He asks them some probing questions about the type of baptism they have received and soon learns that they (like Apollos) have only received "John baptism" (verse 3). Paul explains that John's baptism was meant to lead to the One coming after him who was greater (see John 1:26-27), and that baptism in the Holy Spirit had now been given to all believers. Paul then baptizes them in the name of Jesus, and they also receive the baptism of the Holy Spirit (see verses 4-7).

ERRONEOUS EXORCISMS IN EPHESUS

At the time of Paul, Ephesus (located near present-day Selçuk in Turkey) was one of the largest cities in the Mediterranean world, with a population of more than 400,000. In 27 BC, Emperor Augustus made Ephesus the capital of the province of Asia, and the city had entered into a time of prosperity. It was famed for the Temple of Artemis (Diana), one of the seven wonders of the ancient world, and worship of the goddess permeated all aspects of culture and society in the city.

Paul returns to the synagogue where he has previously taught (see Acts 18:19) and shares the gospel there for three months. When the Jews there, like the ones in Corinth, refuse to listen and speak out against him, Paul moves his base of operations to a lecture hall run by a man named Tyrannus. There he teaches for two years, and God performs many extraordinary miracles through him—the preaching of the word of God and the works of the Holy Spirit go hand in hand (see Acts 19:8-10).

Within the city were a group of men who made a living by invoking the names of a long list of gods to drive out evil spirits in people. Seven sons of a Jewish priest named Sceva were doing this, and they added Jesus' and even Paul's name to the list (see verses 13-14). On one occasion, the demon in a man says to them, "Jesus I know, and Paul I know about, but who are you?" (verse 15). The man then jumps on the seven sons and gives them such a demonically empowered beating that they run out of the house naked and bleeding (see verse 16).

When word of the incident gets out it sparks a revival in the city, and those who had been mixing Christianity with their former occult practices now come forward and confess what they have been doing. Some of these former witches and warlocks burn their occult documents, as they now understand that the power Jesus gives through the Holy Spirit is more powerful than the forces of evil in their city (see verses 17-20).

TAPPING INTO RELIGIOUS PRIDE
Under the guidance of the Holy Spirit, Paul decides to return to the churches he has planted in Macedonia and Asia and then go on to Jerusalem and Rome. One of the reasons he does this at this point is to take up a collection among the Gentile churches for the mother church in Jerusalem. While Luke only briefly mentions this collection (see Acts 24:17), its importance to Paul is such that he refers to it several times in his letters (see Romans 15:25-33; 1 Corinthians 16:1-4; 2 Corinthians 8–9). He prepares for the journey by sending Timothy and another helper, named Erastus, on to Macedonia (see Acts 19:21-22).

As Paul is preparing to leave, a silversmith named Demetrius incites some of his fellow craftsmen to band together and protest what Paul is doing. As previously mentioned, Ephesus was the center of worship of the goddess Artemis, and the craftsmen's business in selling religious trinkets had been affected by the number of people Paul and his band were leading to Christ. Demetrius is able to tap into local religious pride, implying that the city and its famous temple will lose esteem in the eyes of people in the region (see verses 23-27).

People soon begin chanting, "Great is Artemis of the Ephesians!" (Acts 19:28). They drag Gaius and Aristarchus, two of Paul's companions, into an open-air theater commonly found in Greek cities of the time (the one in Ephesus held 25,000 people). This is a frenzied mob, and some of the people caught up in the events are not even sure why they are there. Alexander tries to speak, but he is shouted down by chants that last for two hours (see verses 29-34). Finally, the city clerk gains some sense of order and reminds the Ephesians that because the image of Artemis "fell from heaven" (verse 35), there is no danger of it losing its religious standing.[3] He denies that there are any grounds to prosecute Paul and the others, tells the mob to take its grievances through the established court process, and promptly dismisses the assembly (see verses 36-41).

A WHIRLWIND TOUR

After the uproar in Ephesus, Paul sets out for Macedonia and Greece (see Acts 20:1-2). In 2 Corinthians 2:12, Paul notes that he traveled first to Troas, where he hoped to meet a co-worker named Titus (see map on pages 160-161). A dispute had arisen between him and the church in Corinth, and Paul had sent Titus with a letter to effect reconciliation in preparation for his return. On reaching Macedonia, Paul meets up with Titus, who has a good report for him, and Paul sends him back to Corinth with another letter (see 2 Corinthians 8:16-24). Paul revisits the churches planted in Philippi, Berea and Corinth, where he stays for three months (see Acts 20:2-3).

Eventually, Paul takes the land route back through Macedonia and then sails to Troas. At the same time, Luke reports that he and others set out from Philippi to meet up with them there (see verses 4-6). On the last night of Paul's stay in Troas, he gives a long-winded message that lasts until midnight (which is actually not too uncommon for the time), and this—along with perhaps the odor of the lamps and the stuffiness of the upper room—sends a young boy named Eutychus into a deep sleep. Unfortunately, Eutychus is sitting in a window when he nods off, and he plunges three stories to his death. Paul goes downstairs and, following the method we find Elijah and Elisha using in the Old Testament (see 1 Kings 17:19-23; 2 Kings 4:32-36), throws himself on the young lad. Eutychus returns to life (see Acts 20:7-12).

The next day Paul travels 20 miles to Assos, where he meets up with his companions and boards a ship for Mitylene. They sail to Chios, Samos and Miletus, where he sends for the elders of the church in Ephesus to meet with him. When they arrive, he gives them a farewell address and tells them that the Holy Spirit has compelled him to return to Jerusalem. Paul does not know what will happen to him when he arrives, for in every city he has visited the Holy Spirit has warned him that prison and hardship await him. The elders pray with Paul, weep, embrace him and say their final goodbyes. Paul then boards a ship and sails to Kos, Rhodes and Patara (see Acts 20:13–21:1).

PROPHECY IN TYRE AND CAESAREA

The ship on which Paul is traveling has to unload cargo in Tyre, so Paul takes the opportunity to meet with local believers (see Acts 21:2-3). The believers urge Paul "through the Spirit" not to go to Jerusalem (verse 4), but Paul knows that he has heard directly from the Holy Spirit regarding what he is to do, and he continues on. In the end, it is up to each of us as believers to determine what the Holy Spirit is telling us to do, even though others may hear differently from God about our circumstances.

Arriving in Caesarea, Paul stays at the house of Philip (the one who shared the gospel with the Ethiopian eunuch), where a prophet named Agabus delivers a prophecy to him regarding the manner in which the Jewish leaders in Jerusalem will bind him and hand him over to the Gentiles (see verses 10-11). Interestingly, according to Acts 21:27-33, the Jews did *not* bind Paul (the Roman commander bound him with chains), nor did they hand him over to the Gentiles (the Romans had to forcefully take Paul from the Jews who were trying to kill him)—a point that reveals New Testament prophecy can be accurate on the general level but inaccurate on minor details. As Paul himself noted in 1 Corinthians 14:29-33, all prophecy should be judged and weighed carefully.

When Luke and the others hear this prophecy, they plead with Paul not to go to Jerusalem, but Paul refuses. "Why are you weeping and breaking my heart?" he says to them. "I am ready not only to be bound, but also to die in Jerusalem for the name of the Lord Jesus" (Acts 21:13). Finally, the group sees that Paul will not change his mind, and so they give up and say, "The Lord's will be done" (verse 14). And so, Paul, Luke and the other traveling companions begin to make their way to Jerusalem.

QUESTIONS FOR PERSONAL APPLICATION AND DISCUSSION

It has been said, "You don't become a missionary by crossing the sea; you become a missionary by seeing the cross." What about seeing the cross changed Paul's attitude toward the Mosaic Law?

_____

_____

_____

How was Paul's take on the Law of Moses a radical departure from what went before? Why would traditionalist Jews have thought of Paul as a law-breaker and an apostate Jew?

_____

_____

_____

What was Paul's guiding principle in sharing the gospel? How did that affect which customs he followed when visiting a culture?

_____

_____

_____

_____

_____

What similarities do we find between the demon who possessed the girl in Philippi and the demons who possessed people in the Gospels (see Acts 16:7; Luke 4:34,41; 8:28)?

_____

_____

_____

_____

Why did Paul and Silas insist that the magistrates in Philippi be held accountable for beating and imprisoning them without a trial?

_____

_____

_____

_____

What was unique about the Jews in Berea? What eventually compelled Paul and the others to move from the city?

_____

_____

_____

_____

How did Paul structure his presentation of the gospel to the Athenian philosophers? What does this say about Paul's ability to adapt his message to his audience and situation?

_____

_____

_____

_____

_____

What proclamation did Paul make in Corinth after the Jews there opposed him and became abusive? Did Paul keep to this statement?

_____

_____

_____

_____

What was the problem with the way the sons of Sceva were attempting to cast out evil spirits in people? What occurred as a result? How did this shake up the town of Ephesus?

_____

_____

_____

_____

Luke tells us that believers prophesied "through the Spirit" that Paul should not go to Jerusalem (Acts 21:4). Why did Paul disregard this advice? What does this tell us about prophecy and the work of the Holy Spirit?

_____

_____

_____

_____

Notes

1. After relating the events in Philippi, Luke returns to using the pronoun "they," which indicates that he remained in that city. Because the last place in which we find Paul, Silas and Timothy together is in the home of Lydia, some scholars have speculated that Luke might have married Lydia and settled there.

2. The Oracle of Delphi was actually known as the "Pythia," a name derived from the Greek *pythein* ("to rot"), which refers to the decomposition of the body of Python after it was slain by the Greek god Apollo.

3. The image of Artemis is believed to have been carved from a large meteorite. In ancient times, civilizations often venerated meteorites that fell from the heavens as sacred objects and built shrines around them, the most famous perhaps being the "black stone" of the Ka'aba in Mecca.

Sources

I. Howard Marshall, *The Acts of the Apostles: An Introduction and Commentary,* Tyndale New Testament Commentaries (Grand Rapids, MI: William B. Eerdmans, 1989), pp. 259-342.

Henrietta C. Mears, *What the Bible Is All About,* "Understanding Acts" (Ventura, CA: Regal Books, 2011), chapter 31.

Mears, *Highlights of Scripture, Part Four: Words and Works of Jesus, Teacher's Book* (Los Angeles, CA: The Gospel Light Press, 1937).

C. Peter Wagner, *The Book of Acts: A Commentary* (Ventura, CA: Regal, 2008), pp. 355-466.

AN ODD ENDING
The Holy Spirit in You! (Acts 21:17–28)

SESSION FOCUS
Paul's arrest and trials and his final journey to Rome.

KEY VERSES TO MEMORIZE
The mystery . . . has been kept hidden for ages and generations, but is now disclosed to the Lord's people. To them God has chosen to make known among the Gentiles the glorious riches of this mystery, which is Christ in you, the hope of glory.
COLOSSIANS 1:26-27

WEEKLY READING

DAY 1	Acts 21:17-40
DAY 2	Acts 22:17-30
DAY 3	Acts 23–24
DAY 4	Acts 25; 26:19-32
DAY 5	Acts 27–28

FOR LEADERS: SESSION AT A GLANCE

SESSION OUTLINE	60 MIN.	90 MIN.	WHAT YOU WILL DO
Getting started	10	15	Pray and worship
Main points of the chapter	25	35	Discuss how Jesus is God's Word to us
Application and discussion	15	25	Discuss Paul's arrest, his journey to Rome, and the odd ending to Acts
Looking ahead	5	5	Prepare for next week
Wrapping up	5	10	Close with prayer or song

Jewish Plots and a Roman Arrest

One of the main reasons Paul has returned to Jerusalem is to deliver the collection taken by the Gentile churches in Greece and Asia to help the needy in the city. In Romans 15:31, Paul had expressed his concern that the Jerusalem elders would receive it unfavorably, asking the believers to "pray that I may be kept safe from the unbelievers in Judea and that the contribution I take to Jerusalem may be favorably received by the Lord's people there." Strangely, Luke is almost completely silent on the matter.

Whatever the elders' feelings on the collection, they greet Paul warmly when he arrives and praise God when they hear the report about his work among the Gentiles. But then, almost immediately, they make a request of him. It appears that many of the believers in Jerusalem are still suspicious of Paul and believe that he is encouraging Jewish believers in Gentile areas to abandon the customs of Judaism. To prove to these believers that Paul is on the up and up, the elders ask him to sponsor four men in taking a Nazarite vow—and take part in the purification rites—which Paul agrees to do (see Acts 21:17-25).

PAUL'S ARREST

The trouble for Paul begins when he visits the Temple at the end of the seven-day purification process. There, some Jews from the province of Asia (Ephesus) see him and begin to stir up the crowd against him, claiming that he had brought Gentiles into the Temple. A mob forms and attempts to kill Paul on the spot, but a Roman commander named Claudius Lysias intervenes and has Paul led away in chains (see Acts 21:27-36).

At first the commander thinks Paul is one of the fugitives from justice for whom he and his agents had been searching, but Paul soon clears up the misunderstanding. At this point, he asks to speak to the people, and Lysias grants his request (see verses 37-40). This begins the first of Paul's three "defenses" of his actions (see 22:1-21; 24:10-21; 26:1-23). This final account of Paul's imprisonment and trials in Jerusalem and Caesarea, and his subsequent journey to Rome, take up a quarter of the book of Acts, which reveals the importance that Luke placed on these events.

PAUL'S DEFENSE TO THE JERUSALEM CROWD

Paul begins his speech by addressing the mob in the same manner as Stephen: "Brothers and fathers, listen now to my defense" (Acts 22:1; see also 7:2). When the crowd hears him speak in Aramaic and not in Greek, they begin to settle down. Paul speaks as a Jew to Jews. He begins by affirming that he is a loyal Jew—trained at the feet of Gamaliel—who had a zeal for persecuting the early Jesus movement. Paul goes on to recount his conversion experience (see Acts 9:1-19), adding the additional details that his blinding on the road to Damascus occurred at noon (see Acts 22:6) and that after he heard Jesus' voice, he asked, "What shall I do, Lord?" (verse 10). Paul also mentions that Ananias was "a devout observer of the law and highly respected by all the Jews living there" (verse 12), which would have appealed to this particular audience.

Following the explanation of his conversion, Paul adds an additional account not found in Luke's prior version. He states that he went to the Temple (which, once again, would have been significant to this crowd), where he had a second vision of Jesus. The Lord told him to take the message to the Gentiles, for the people of Jerusalem would not accept the message of the Messiah (see verses 17-21). At this, the crowd erupts and calls for Paul's death. Lysias, perplexed at what is occurring, orders Paul to be flogged and interrogated, but Paul halts this by telling the commander that he is a Roman citizen and thus has rights (see verses 22-29).

PAUL'S DEFENSE BEFORE THE SANHEDRIN

Lysias still wants to know why the Jews are so upset with Paul, so he orders the chief priests and the members of the Sanhedrin to gather. The meeting doesn't start well. Paul begins by telling the council that he stands blameless before God. Ananias, the high priest (appointed in AD 47), perceives this to be a lie and orders those standing near Paul to hit him in the mouth (see Acts 23:1-2). Paul, apparently not realizing Ananias is the high priest, says, "God will strike you, you whitewashed wall!" (Acts 23:3). Given Ananias's record of corruption in office and his brutal death some years later in AD 66, Luke's readers would have perceived this as a prophecy come true.[1]

Paul apologizes for his outburst, stating that he did not realize Ananias was the high priest, and quotes a passage from Exodus 22:28 to show that he knows the law about speaking ill of "the ruler of your people" (Acts 23:5). He then goes on to subtly instigate a dispute among the factions of the council (the Sadducees and Pharisees) over the issue of the resurrection of the dead, and the debate gets so heated that Lysias fears Paul will be torn to pieces and takes him back to the Roman barracks (see verses 6-10).

Trial in Caesarea

The next morning, some 40 Jews form a conspiracy to have Paul killed and agree to go on a hunger strike until the deed is done. Fortunately, Paul's nephew (the first and last we will hear of this individual) discovers the plot. The young man tells the Roman commander Lysias that the Jews are planning to ask him to bring Paul back before the Sanhedrin, where they will ambush and kill him. Lysias tells the boy not to mention what he knows to anyone, and then he quietly orders a force of 470 soldiers to escort Paul to Caesarea. Lysias will now hand Paul over to his superior, Marcus Antonius Felix, the governor of the region (see Acts 23:12-24).

TERTULLUS THE LAWYER

Lysias sends a letter to Felix explaining the situation, but he provides no formal accusation against Paul. Felix, for his part, follows the proper protocol and conducts a brief interrogation in which he establishes Paul's Roman citizenship and province of birth. Felix then agrees to hear his case—*after* the Jewish leaders in Jerusalem arrive to state their claims against him. In the meantime, Felix provides Paul with some nice accommodations in Herod's palace and places him under house arrest (see Acts 23:25-35).

The high priest, Ananias, and a lawyer named Tertullus arrive five days later. Tertullus begins by flattering the governor, telling him that the nation has enjoyed "a long period of peace" under him (Acts 24:2)—a not-quite truth, as Felix's reign had been characterized by unrest, and relations between the Romans and Jews had deteriorated. Tertullus then makes his case against Paul: (1) he is a troublemaker (a "pestilent fellow" in the *KJV*), (2) the ringleader of a Nazarene sect, and (3) has attempted to desecrate the Temple. Felix nods to Paul and allows him to make his defense (see Acts 24:1-10).

Paul denies that he is a troublemaker and notes that Tertullus has provided no witness to prove this claim against him. He admits to be a follower of "the Way," but states that Christians still regard the Law and the Prophets as God's word (in fact, they see Jesus as being the fulfillment of Old Testament prophecy). Paul also denies desecrating the Temple, reminding the group that he in fact was performing a purification ritual according to Jewish law when he was arrested (see verses 10-21).

After hearing the charges and Paul's defense, Felix decides to defer making a decision until he can speak with the Roman commander Lysias. He has heard about "the Way" and is apparently curious about it, so he calls Paul in several days later to explain more about Jesus and the gospel. When Paul gets to the uncomfortable parts about righteousness, self-control and judgment, Felix, who has no intention of repenting, decides he has heard enough and sends Paul back to house arrest. He is hoping that Paul will offer him a bribe to set him free, but this doesn't happen (see verses 22-26).

An Appeal to Caesar

Felix is governor of Judea from AD 52–58, and he leaves Paul in prison for two years to curry favor with the Jews, whom he needs to have on his side to ensure order in the region. He is succeeded by Porcius Festus, who takes over all of the problems that Felix had left (see Acts 24:27). During this time, the members of the Sanhedrin do not forget about Paul. As soon as Festus comes into office, they again present their charges against Paul and ask the new governor to transfer him to Jerusalem for trial (see Acts 25:1-9).

Paul is no fool—this same group has previously plotted his death—and so he chooses to take his chances in a Roman court. As a Roman citizen, he has the right of *provocatio,* in which he can make an "appeal to Caesar" and have his case referred to Rome, and this is what he does (see verses 10-11). Festus confers with his legal experts to make sure this specific procedure applies in this case, and then announces, "You have appealed to Caesar. To Caesar you will go!" (Acts 24:12).

A Visit from Herod Agrippa II

A few days later, Festus receives a state visit from Herod Agrippa II (the son of Herod Agrippa, who had executed John the Baptist and the disciple James) and Bernice, the king's younger sister. Festus tells Agrippa all about Paul, which sparks the king's curiosity. The next day, during a formal procession in which Paul is brought before Agrippa and Bernice, Festus admits to being in a bit of a quandary as to what formal charges against Paul to make to Rome. He hopes that Agrippa can help him out (see Acts 25:13-27).

Paul's speech to Agrippa is similar to the other speeches he has made in this section of Acts. He begins by referring to his way of life in his youth as if it were universally known, and he goes on to recount his conversion experience (see Acts 26:2-18). Unique to this version are that all of Paul's companions fell to the ground after seeing the light, that Jesus spoke to him in Aramaic (see verse 14), and the additional comments that Christ makes to him (see verses 16-18).

Festus is not well versed in all aspects of Jewish theology, and when Paul relates the prophecies concerning the Messiah rising from the dead, he calls Paul insane (see verse 24). Paul denies the charge, but his subsequent question to Agrippa puts the king in a tough spot: "Do you believe the prophets? I know you do" (verse 27). If Agrippa answers yes, the necessary conclusion would be that Jesus is the Messiah; if he answers no, he would offend the Jewish establishment. So he avoids the question and says, "Do you think that in such a short time you can persuade me to be a Christian?" (verse 28).

The assembly is dismissed, Paul is led back in chains, and Agrippa, Festus and Bernice begin discussing his case.[2] They all agree that Paul has done nothing worthy of death or imprisonment, but because he has appealed to Caesar, he must remain a prisoner until his trial in Rome. Paul will soon be sailing to Italy (see verses 30-32).

Danger on the High Seas

When the action picks up in Acts 27, Luke has again joined Paul (the last time he used "we" was when Paul and the others arrived in Jerusalem, but before Paul's meeting before the Sanhedrin). Some have speculated that Luke might have been present in Caesarea during Paul's two-year imprisonment working on his Gospel and Acts, or he might have been back home in Philippi. In any event, he will accompany Paul to Rome.

In ancient times, sailors avoided making journeys in winter and sailed close to the coastline of the Mediterranean Sea to avoid storms in the area. This "prison ship" follows that course, hopping from port to port "along the coast of the province of Asia" (Acts 27:2). Aristarchus, who Paul notes in Colossians 4:10 was a fellow prisoner, is also with him on the journey (see also Philemon 1:24).

From Caesarea, the ship travels north to Sidon, north and west around the isle of Cyprus, and then west to Myra (see map on pages 160-161). At this time there was an important trade route from Egypt to Rome, and the centurion in charge is able to secure passage on one of these vessels coming from Alexandria, which would have been larger and more suited to the journey. Unfortunately, there is a prevailing northwesterly wind, and the ship struggles to make it to Cnidus, located on the tip of Asia Minor, and then on to an open harbor known as Fair Havens, a harbor on the southern coast of the island of Crete (see Acts 27:3-8).

THE STORM

Winter was approaching, and Paul could see that conditions for sailing were getting dangerous. He had likely also received a prophetic word from God that the voyage would end in peril, and so he tells the centurion, "I can see that our voyage is going to be disastrous and bring great loss to ship and cargo, and to our own lives also" (Acts 27:10). The Roman centurion likely defers to the opinion of the pilot and owner of the ship, who decide to journey the short distance to the port of Phoenix (see verses 11-12).

It soon becomes clear that this is a bad decision. A hurricane-force wind (known as a *Euraquilo*) sweeps down from Crete. Ancient ships could not tack (a technique for sailing into the wind) or face rough seas, so the vessel is caught by the storm and pushed into the sea. The sailors are barely able to secure the small lifeboat typically dragged behind the ship and fasten ropes under the ship to hold the craft together. By the next day, the crew is throwing cargo overboard, probably because the ship is taking on water and they need to lighten the load. The sailors now have no idea where they are, and the storm prevents them from seeing sun, stars or shoreline (see verses 13-20).

THE SHIPWRECK

At this point when all hope is lost, Paul relates to them a prophetic word from God that he has received. He tells the sailors that the ship will be lost, but all lives on board will be saved. Two weeks after sailing from Fair Havens, the ship hits shallow waters. Some of the sailors attempt to escape from the ship, but Paul tells the centurion that for the prophecy he delivered to come to pass, *everyone* must stay on board. This time the centurion listens to him, and the lifeboats are cut free (see Acts 27:21-32).

After sharing a meal and again lightening the load, the sailors spot a sandy beach and attempt to run the ship aground on it. The maneuver fails and the ship hits a sandbar and is broken apart. In the confusion the Roman soldiers plan to kill the prisoners to keep them from escaping, but the centurion wants to spare Paul's life and thus keeps them from carrying out this action. So he orders those who can swim to make their way to land and the others to climb onto planks. When they all make it to shore, they discover that they are on the island of Malta (see Acts 27:33–Acts 28:1).

THE SNAKEBITE

On the island Paul is apparently given freedom to move around, and he helps in gathering wood for a fire. As he lays a pile of brushwood on the fire,

a viper suddenly darts out and bites his hand. While it is not clear if the
snake was poisonous (there are no venomous snakes on the island today),
the native Maltans believe it is, and they comment that Paul must have
done something to earn this cruel twist of fate. However, Paul shakes off the
snake and goes on his way (see Acts 28:2-6). In this event, Paul seems to be
living out the words that Jesus spoke in Mark 16:16-18: "These signs will accompany those who believe: In my name they will drive out demons; they
will speak in new tongues; they will pick up snakes with their hands."

The Odd Ending

After spending three months on Malta, the weather finally clears up
enough for grain ships sailing from Egypt to reach the island. Paul and
the others are put aboard a ship and sail from Malta north to Sicily and
then up the western coast of Italy, putting in at various ports along the
way. At long last, Paul reaches Rome, where he is put under house arrest.
Three days later, he calls together the local Jewish leaders and explains why
he is in Rome and the charges the Jews in Jerusalem and Asia made against
him (see Acts 28:11-20).

The Jews remark that they have not received any letters from Judea
about Paul, but that they have heard much about the early Jesus movement and want to know more. In this way, Paul is able to share the gospel
among them and how Jesus fulfilled Old Testament prophecy. As usual,
some come to believe in Christ, but others reject Paul's message (see verses
21-24). Paul's final words sum up Luke's main theme that he has stressed
throughout the book of Acts: "Therefore I want you to know that God's
salvation has been sent to the Gentiles, and they will listen!" (verse 28).

WHAT HAPPENED TO THOSE IN THE EARLY CHURCH?
With the exception of John the Baptist, James and Stephen, the book of
Acts does not tell us what happened to Jesus' original disciples, or to the
other prominent leaders in the early Jesus movement, or even to Paul him-
self. The reason for this is simple: Luke ended his story of Paul in AD 63,
and many of these early leaders had not yet been martyred for their faith.
For this reason, we need to turn to other sources such as Hippolytus of
Rome (AD 170–236), Eusebius (AD 263–339) and Early Church traditions.
While it is not certain if these early writings are completely accurate, they
often provide our "best guess" of what happened to these individuals.

Based on these sources, here is a summary of what happened to many of the leaders in the early Jesus movement (note that there are varying accounts of their ministry regions and deaths):

NAME	POSITION	MINISTRY REGION	DEATH
Andrew	Disciple	Sythia and Thrace	Crucified on X-shaped cross in Patrae (Greece)
Bartholomew	Disciple	India	Crucified head-downward in Allanum (Georgia)
James, the Son of Alphaeus	Disciple	Judea and Egypt	Died by stoning in Jerusalem
John	Disciple/ Writer	Judea and Ephesus	Banished to Isle of Patmos and later died in Ephesus (the only disciple not to be martyred)
Judas, son of James (Thaddaeus)	Disciple	Edessa and Mesopotamia	Martyred in Berytus (Lebanon)
Matthew (Levi)	Disciple/ Writer	Judea and Parthia	Died in Hierees in Parthia (Iran)
Peter (Simon)	Disciple	Judea	Crucified head-downward in Rome
Philip	Disciple	Greece, Syria and Phrygia	Crucified head-downward in Hierapolis (Turkey)
Simon the Zealot	Disciple	Middle East and Africa	Possibly sawn in half in Persia (Iran)
Thomas (Didymus)	Disciple	Parthia, Persia, Hyrcania, Bactria, India	Killed with a pine spear in India
Matthias	Disciple (replaced Judas)	Judea, Ethiopia and Colchis	Crucified in Colchis (Georgia)
Mary Magdalene	Early leader	Judea and Ephesus	Died in Ephesus
Mary of Bethany	Early leader	Mediterranean region	Died in Cyprus (along with Lazarus and Martha)

NAME	POSITION	MINISTRY REGION	DEATH
Paul	Apostle	Mediterranean region	Beheaded in Rome
James "the Just"	Leader of Jerusalem church	Judea	Died by stoning in Jerusalem
Barnabas	Apostle	Mediterranean region	Martyred at Salamis (Cyprus)
Silas	Early leader	Mediterranean region	Martyred in Macedonia
John Mark	Writer	Mediterranean region and Africa	Hung in Alexandria (Egypt)
Timothy	Early leader	Mediterranean region	Died by stoning in Ephesus
Luke	Writer	Mediterranean region	Died in Boeotia (Greece)

From this information, we can see that these leaders in the Early Church (1) followed Jesus' command to go "to the ends of the earth" (Acts 1:8), and (2) understood that they would have trouble in this world (and face martyrdom). Each of these disciples, apostles and leaders in the Jesus movement were willing to die for the sake of sharing the gospel to the world.

THE "MORE" OF ACTS

After all the big outpourings of the Holy Spirit, the miracles, the dramatic escapes from death, the amazing breakthroughs to the Gentiles, and Paul's appeal to Caesar and twists and turns on his journey to Rome, the book of Acts ends abruptly: "For two whole years Paul stayed there in his own rented house and welcomed all who came to see him. He proclaimed the kingdom of God and taught about the Lord Jesus Christ—with all boldness and without hindrance!" (Acts 28:30-31).

The ending doesn't close the circle, and there's an unfinished quality about it. There are too many loose ends that haven't been tied together. The mission to the Gentiles has been left hanging. Paul's voyage was made as a result of his appealing to Caesar, but he has not met Caesar. Paul (and we the readers) is left in two years of suspense, waiting for something to happen, with no resolution. What's next? We want more! The "more" is our story. We who believe in the testimony of those who went before us—many, as we have seen, who died for Jesus—are the ones who complete this story. Filled with the Holy Spirit, we are "Acts 29."

QUESTIONS FOR PERSONAL APPLICATION AND DISCUSSION

The collection for Jerusalem was a major theme in many of Paul's letters. Why do you think Luke makes only a passing reference to it?

_____

_____

_____

_____

_____

What led to Paul's arrest in the Temple? How does Paul appeal to his Jewish audience in making his defense?

_____

_____

_____

_____

What charges does Tertullus make against Paul? Why does Paul make an appeal to Caesar—and thus ensure that he will have a trial in Rome?

_____

_____

_____

_____

What was Festus hoping to achieve by telling Herod Agrippa about Paul? What was Agrippa's reaction?

_____

_____

_____

What similarities do you notice between Paul's trials in Acts and Jesus' trials in Luke's Gospel (see Luke 23)? What differences do you notice?

_____

_____

_____

_____

_____

During the journey to Rome, Paul received a prophetic word from God while the ship was anchored at Fair Havens that could have prevented a disaster. Why did the Roman commander, the pilot and the owner of the ship ignore him?

_____

_____

_____

_____

_____

What prophetic word did Paul deliver to the Roman commander while the ship was in the storm? What was the centurion's response?

_____

_____

_____

_____

_____

What happened to most of the leaders in the Early Church? What does this say about their faith and the conviction they had that Jesus was "the way and the truth and the life" (John 14:6)?

_____

_____

_____

_____

_____

Throughout the book of Acts we see that believers assisted Paul in every aspect of his ministry—he did not do it alone. What does this tell you about how missions work should be done today? How can you better support missions in your local area as well as overseas?

Because of the prominence of the Holy Spirit in the book of Acts, the supernatural is very much a part of the story. What parts of the story of the Early Church leap to your mind as you think about the big picture of the book of Acts?

Notes

1. Ananias ruled as high priest from AD 48 to 59. Josephus writes that he embezzled tithes given to the priests and gave bribes to Romans and Jews. He was a brutal and scheming man, and the Jewish nationalists despised him for his loyalties with Rome. When the Jewish-Roman war broke out in AD 66, the nationalists burned his house, forcing him to flee to the palace of Herod the Great. There he hid in an aqueduct on the palace grounds, but he was discovered and put to death.
2. Of course, neither Luke nor Paul would have been present at this discussion. It is likely that information indicating that Agrippa, Festus and Bernice discussed Paul's case was sent with the centurion who escorted Paul to Rome.

Sources

I. Howard Marshall, *The Acts of the Apostles: An Introduction and Commentary,* Tyndale New Testament Commentaries (Grand Rapids, MI: William B. Eerdmans, 1989), pp. 342-427.

Henrietta C. Mears, *What the Bible Is All About,* "Understanding Acts" (Ventura, CA: Regal Books, 2011), chapter 31.

Mears, *Highlights of Scripture, Part Four: Words and Works of Jesus, Teacher's Book* (Los Angeles, CA: The Gospel Light Press, 1937).

C. Peter Wagner, *The Book of Acts: A Commentary* (Ventura, CA: Regal, 2008), pp. 467-496.

THE MEDITERRANEAN REGION

AT THE TIME OF PAUL (C. AD 70)

THRACE

Byzantium

Neapolis

BITHYNIA
AND PONTUS

Trapezus

CAPPADOCIA

Samothrace

Nicaea

MYSIA

GALATIA

Troas

Ancyra

Assos

Adramyttium

ASIA

Caesarea

Pergamum

Thyatira

Mitylene

Pisidian
Antioch

Smyrna

Sardis

Philadelphia

Chios

Iconium

CILICIA

LYDIA

Laodicia

Colosse

PISIDIA

Ephesus

Derbe

Samos

Miletus

PHRYGIA

Lystra

Tarsus

Patmos

CARIA

PAMPHYLIA

Antioch

Cos

Perga

Selucia
Pieria

LYCIA

Attalia

SYRIA

Cnidus

Rhodes

Patara

Myra

CRETE

Salamis

asea

Cape Salmone

Fair Havens

Paphos

CYPRUS

Sidon

Damascus

Tyre

Ptolemais

Nazareth

Caesarea

JUDEA

Jerusalem

Paraetonium

Alexandria

EGYPT

ARABIA

• Major Roman/biblical city   ★ City/area visited by Paul   - - - Roman province

A TIMELINE OF ACTS

Date (ad)	Source	Event
Spring 32	Acts 1	On Passover of this year, Jesus is crucified and raised from the dead. He gives His followers the Great Commission and then ascends into heaven.
	Acts 2	On the Day of Pentecost, the Church is born in Jerusalem, the Holy Spirit is poured out, Peter preaches his first sermon and 3,000 come to believe.
	Acts 3	Peter heals a crippled man. This leads to Peter's second sermon, illustrating how the Hebrew Bible was used in the Early Church to show that Jesus fulfilled biblical prophecies.
	Acts 4	The number of believers in Jesus swells to 5,000, upsetting the religious establishment. Peter and John are arrested, questioned, threatened and released.
	Acts 5	Ananias and Sapphira try (and fail) to deceive the Church. The apostles are arrested, escape, arrested again and defy the council. They are furious, but Gamaliel calms them down. The apostles are flogged and released. The believers keep proclaiming in the Temple precincts and houses.

DATE (AD)	SOURCE	EVENT
Spring 32	Acts 6	Stephen is appointed to oversee the daily distribution of food to widows. He performs miracles in Jesus' name and is arrested and brought before the Sanhedrin.
	Acts 7	Stephen acts in his own defense. He tells the well-known story of Israel—of God's leading and grace and of the peoples' stubbornness. Just before he "falls asleep," Stephen sees Jesus standing at God's right hand.
	Acts 8	Saul starts a campaign of repression against the believers, and they are scattered in many directions. Philip preaches in Samaria, baptizes new believers, and starts Jesus-fellowships. Philip also leads an Ethiopian eunuch to Christ.
37–40	Acts 9; 2 Cor. 11:32; Gal. 1:17-18	The risen Jesus meets Saul on his way to persecute the believers in Damascus. Saul is converted. Tiberius Caesar dies and King Aretas IV takes over Damascus. The disciples learn of a plot against Paul's life. King Aretas sets up a dragnet to catch Paul, but he escapes in a basket lowered from the city wall. Paul lays low in Arabia for three years. King Aretas dies. Paul returns to Damascus and meets with the apostles and Barnabas in Jerusalem. Paul preaches boldly in Jerusalem, but some Hellenized Jews try to kill him. Paul escapes to his hometown of Tarsus.

DATE (AD)	SOURCE	EVENT
37–40	Acts 10	Cornelius the Gentile God-fearer and Peter the Hebraic Jewish believer in Jesus have near-simultaneous visions from the Lord. Peter goes to Cornelius's house and preaches the gospel. Everyone believes, receives the Holy Spirit and is baptized.
43–44	Acts 11	Peter justifies his actions to the mother church in Jerusalem. A Jewish-Gentile church begins in Syrian Antioch. Barnabas is sent there, and he gets Paul in Tarsus and brings him to Antioch. They teach there for a year. The believers in Antioch are first called Christians. A famine strikes Judea; the church in Antioch sends relief via Paul, Barnabas and Mark.
	Acts 12	Herod Agrippa kills James, the brother of John. Peter is arrested and miraculously escapes from prison. Herod Agrippa dies. Paul, Barnabas and Mark return to Antioch from their relief mission due to the famine in Judea.
46	Acts 13	Paul goes on his first missions trip with Barnabas. They sail from Seleucia to the island of Cyprus, visiting Salamos and Paphos. From Cyprus they sail to Perga and move inland to Pisidian Antioch. They meet stiff opposition in Iconium. An attempt is made on Paul's life in Lystra, but he survives.

DATE (AD)	SOURCE	EVENT
Before 50	Acts 14	Paul and Barnabas retrace the path of their mission through Pisidian Antioch back to their home church in Antioch. The first missionary journey ends with Paul and Barnabas giving a full report to the church in Antioch.
50	Acts 15; Gal. 2:1-9	The Jerusalem Council is held (this happens 14 years after Paul's conversion). Paul and Barnabas have a dispute. Paul and Silas go to Syria and Cicilia, while Barnabas and Mark go to Cyprus.
Spring 51	Acts 16	Paul's second missionary trip begins. The Holy Spirit prevents Paul and Silas from going to Bithynia. Paul gets a vision from the Holy Spirit to go to Macedonia. They itinerate through northern Greece, including starting a church in Philippi.
Winter/ Spring 52	Acts 17	Paul and Silas move southward in Greece to Thessalonica, Berea and Athens. Paul preaches to the philosophers at the Aereopagus. A few believe.
Spring 52– Fall 53	Acts 18	Paul goes to Corinth and stays there 18 months. He writes 1 and 2 Thessalonians. He crosses the Aegean Sea to Ephesus and finishes his second missionary journey in Antioch. He begins his third missionary journey. Meanwhile, Apollos preaches in Ephesus.
52 or 53	Seutonius, *The Twelve Caesars*	Emperor Claudius Caesar banishes all Jews from Rome.

DATE (AD)	SOURCE	EVENT
Spring 54	Acts 19	Paul preaches and does miracles in Ephesus. The city's silversmiths start a riot in the name of Artemis (Diana). The city clerk manages to disperse the unruly crowd.
Fall 54–Fall 57	Acts 20	Paul writes 1 and 2 Corinthians, Romans and Galatians. He continues his third missionary journey (retracing the steps of the second missionary journey). He raises a young man from the dead in Troas. Paul stays in Ephesus for three years and gives a farewell speech to the believers.
57	Tacitus, *Annals*	Pomponia Graecina, wife of Plautius (who led the Roman conquest of Britain in AD 43), is accused of some superstition and handed over to her husband's judicial decision.
58	Acts 21	Paul's third missionary journey ends in Jerusalem. He delivers the collection from the Gentile churches to James. Paul takes a vow to show he is still Jewish. Jews from Asia Minor see him in the Temple and stir up the crowd against him. A Roman commander arrests him. The risen Jesus tells Paul he will testify about Him in Rome.
	Acts 22	Paul defends himself before the angry mob in Jerusalem. He tells the commander he is a Roman citizen and avoids a flogging.

DATE (AD)	SOURCE	EVENT
58	Acts 23	Paul addresses the Sanhedrin. A plot is discovered of assassins who have taken a vow to kill Paul. The Roman commander sends Paul under heavy guard to Governor Felix.
58–60	Acts 24	Paul is taken to Caesarea and defends himself before Governor Felix. Felix keeps Paul under guard for two years. Festus replaces Felix and, as a favor to the Jews against Paul, decides to leave Paul in prison.
60	Acts 25	Festus's reign begins. Paul appeals to Caesar. Festus sends Paul to Herod Agrippa, who interviews Paul.
	Acts 26	Paul makes his defense to Herod Agrippa.
	Acts 27	Paul, as a prisoner, is sent to Rome. Luke and Aristarchus are with him. They are caught in a storm and shipwrecked. Paul prophesies that they will all live.
Winter 60–62	Acts 28; Eph. 1:1; 3:1; 4:1; 6:20; Phil. 1:1,7; 4:23; Col. 1:1; 4:10,18; Philem. 1:1	The ship is wrecked on Malta. A snake, whom the Maltans believe to be poisonous bites Paul, but he lives. He finally arrives in Rome and spends two years under house arrest. During this time, he writes Ephesians, Colossians, Philemon and Philippians.

DATE (AD)	SOURCE	EVENT
63	Rom. 1:10; Phil. 1:26; 15:24,28; 16:1, 3,5; Col. 4:9-14; 2 Tim. 4:13, 20; Titus 1:5; 3:12; Philem. 1:2, 9-10,22-25	Paul is released from prison and possibly visits Colosse, Philippi, Spain, Corinth, Troas, Crete and Nicopolis.
Summer 64	Tacitus, *Annals*	Emperor Nero starts a fire in AD 64 and blames it on the Christians. He begins to round up Christians and have them put to death.
	Clement, *Stromateus*	Nero kills Peter and Peter's wife.
64–65	Heb. 13:23-24	Timothy is released from prison. Paul writes 1 Timothy and possibly Hebrews. Paul is still free.
Fall 66		Paul is put in prison, awaiting death. He writes 2 Timothy.
66–67	Clement, *Letter to the Corinthians*	Nero has Paul beheaded.

LEADER'S TIPS

The following are some general guidelines for leaders to follow when using the *What the Bible Is All About* Bible Studies with a small group. Note that each of the sessions are designed to be used in either 60-minute or 90-minute meetings (see the overview page for a session outline). Generally, the ideal size for group is between 10 to 20 people, which is small enough for meaningful fellowship but large enough for dynamic group interaction. It is typically best to stop opening up the group to members after the second session and invite them to join the next study after the 12 weeks are complete.

GROUP DYNAMICS
Getting a group of people actively involved in discussing issues of the Christian life is highly worthwhile. Not only does group interaction help to create interest, stimulate thinking and encourage effective learning, but it is also vital for building quality relationships within the group. Only as people begin to share their thoughts and feelings will they begin to build bonds of friendship and support.

However, some people resist participating in groups that feature interaction—and with good reason. Discussions can can get off-track, and group members may have opinions and feelings without having any solid knowledge of the topic. Sometimes, members may worry that they will be expected to talk about matters that will make them feel awkward, and some members might be intimidated into silence. Opening up the floor for comments from individuals may result in disagreements being aired, and issues may end up being "resolved" by majority opinion rather than on knowledgeable grounds.

Granted, some people will prefer to bypass any group participation and get right to the content ("I just want to study the Bible—I don't have time to get to know a bunch of strangers"). However, it is never possible to effectively separate knowledge and love. Information without relationship is sterile, and truth apart from touch will turn to untruth. For this reason, while group interaction may at times seem difficult and even non-productive, leaders and group members can work together to achieve positive results.

LEADING THE GROUP
The following tips can be helpful in making group interaction a positive learning opportunity for everyone:

- When a question or comment is raised that is off the subject, either suggest that it be dealt with at another time or ask the group if they would prefer to pursue the new issue at that time.

- When someone talks too much, direct a few questions specifically to other people, making sure not to put any shy people on the spot. Talk privately with the "dominator" and ask for cooperation in helping to draw out the quieter group members.

- When someone does not participate verbally, assign a few questions to be discussed in pairs, trios or other small groups, or distribute paper and pencil and invite people to write their answer to a specific question or two. Then invite several people (including the quiet ones) to read what they wrote.

- If someone asks a question that you don't know how to answer, admit it and move on. If the question calls for insight about personal experience, invite group members to comment. If the question requires specialized knowledge, offer to look for an answer before the next session (make sure to follow up the next session).

- When group members disagree with you or each other, remind them that it is possible to disagree without becoming disagreeable. To help clarify the issues while maintaining a climate of mutual acceptance, encourage those on opposite sides to restate what they have heard the other person(s) saying about the issue. Then invite each side to evaluate how accurately they feel their position was presented. Ask group members to identify as many points as possible related to the topic on which both sides agree, and then lead the group in examining other Scriptures related to the topic, looking for common ground that they can all accept.

- Finally, urge group members to keep an open heart and mind and a willingness to continue loving one another while learning more about the topic at hand.

If the disagreement involves an issue on which your church has stated a position, be sure that stance is clearly and positively presented. This should be done not to squelch dissent but to ensure there is no confusion over where your church stands.

ONE-YEAR BIBLE READING PLAN

✔	By the End of ...	Read Through These Passages ...		
		Books of Law and History	Books of Poetry and Prophecy	New Testament Books
	Month 1	Genesis 1– Genesis 37	Job 1– Job 42	Matthew 1– Matthew 20
	Month 2	Genesis 38– Exodus 25	Psalm 1– Psalm 62	Matthew 21– Mark 8
	Month 3	Exodus 26– Leviticus 23	Psalm 63– Psalm 117	Mark 9– Luke 6
	Month 4	Leviticus 24– Numbers 28	Psalm 118– Proverbs 18	Luke 7– Luke 24
	Month 5	Numbers 29– Deuteronomy 30	Proverbs 19– Isaiah 8	John 1– John 13
	Month 6	Deuteronomy 31– Judges 8	Isaiah 9– Isaiah 43	John 14– Acts 11
	Month 7	Judges 9– 1 Samuel 21	Isaiah 44– Jeremiah 6	Acts 12– Romans 1
	Month 8	1 Samuel 22– 1 Kings 2	Jeremiah 7– Jeremiah 38	Romans 2- 1 Corinthians 11
	Month 9	1 Kings 3– 2 Kings 10	Jeremiah 39– Ezekiel 15	1 Corinthians 12– Ephesians 6
	Month 10	2 Kings 11– 1 Chronicles 17	Ezekiel 16– Ezekiel 45	Philippians 1– Philemon
	Month 11	1 Chronicles 18– 2 Chronicles 31	Ezekiel 46– Amos 6	Hebrews 1– 2 Peter 3
	Month 12	2 Chronicles 32– Esther 10	Amos 7– Malachi 4	1 John 1– Revelation 22

TWO-YEAR BIBLE READING PLAN

✔	BY THE END OF . . .	READ THROUGH THESE PASSAGES . . .		
		BOOKS OF LAW AND HISTORY	BOOKS OF POETRY AND PROPHECY	NEW TESTAMENT BOOKS
	Month 1	Genesis 1– Genesis 21	Job 1– Job 20	Matthew 1– Matthew 11
	Month 2	Genesis 32– Genesis 37	Job 21– Job 42	Matthew 12– Matthew 20
	Month 3	Genesis 38– Exodus 6	Psalm 1– Psalm 33	Matthew 21– Matthew 28
	Month 4	Exodus 7– Exodus 25	Psalm 34– Psalm 62	Mark 1– Mark 8
	Month 5	Exodus 26– Leviticus 5	Psalm 63– Psalm 88	Mark 9– Mark 16
	Month 6	Leviticus 6– Leviticus 23	Psalm 89– Psalm 117	Luke 1– Luke 6
	Month 7	Leviticus 24– Numbers 11	Psalm 118– Psalm 150	Luke 7– Luke 13
	Month 8	Numbers 12– Numbers 28	Proverbs 1– Proverbs 18	Luke 14– Luke 24
	Month 9	Numbers 29– Deuteronomy 9	Proverbs 19– Ecclesiastes 7	John 1– John 6
	Month 10	Deuteronomy 10– Deuteronomy 30	Ecclesiastes 8– Isaiah 8	John 7– John 13
	Month 11	Deuteronomy 31– Joshua 14	Isaiah 9– Isaiah 27	John 14– Acts 2
	Month 12	Joshua 15– Judges 8	Isaiah 28– Isaiah 43	Acts 3– Acts 11
	Month 13	Judges 9– 1 Samuel 2	Isaiah 44– Isaiah 59	Acts 12– Acts 20
	Month 14	1 Samuel 3– 1 Samuel 21	Isaiah 60– Jeremiah 6	Acts 21– Acts 28
	Month 15	1 Samuel 22– 2 Samuel 12	Jeremiah 7– Jeremiah 23	Romans 1– Romans 13
	Month 16	2 Samuel 13– 1 Kings 2	Jeremiah 24– Jeremiah 38	Romans 14– 1 Corinthians 11
	Month 17	1 Kings 3– 1 Kings 16	Jeremiah 39– Jeremiah 52	1 Corinthians 12– 2 Corinthians 10
	Month 18	1 Kings 17– 2 Kings 10	Lamentations 1– Ezekiel 15	2 Corinthians 11– Ephesians 6
	Month 19	2 Kings 11– 2 Kings 25	Ezekiel 16– Ezekiel 29	Philippians 1– 1 Thessalonians 5
	Month 20	1 Chronicles 1– 1 Chronicles 17	Ezekiel 30– Ezekiel 45	2 Thessalonians 1– Philemon
	Month 21	1 Chronicles 18– 2 Chronicles 8	Ezekiel 46– Daniel 12	Hebrews 1– Hebrews 13
	Month 22	2 Chronicles 9– 2 Chronicles 31	Hosea 1– Amos 6	James 1– 2 Peter 3
	Month 23	2 Chronciles 32– Nehemiah 3	Amos 7– Habakkuk 3	1 John 1– Revelation 9
	Month 24	Nehemiah 4– Esther 10	Zephaniah 1– Malachi 4	Revelation 10– Revelation 22

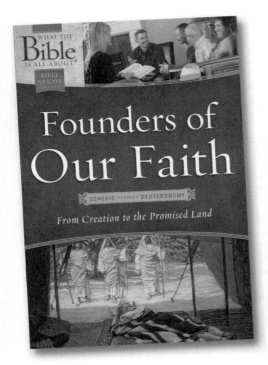
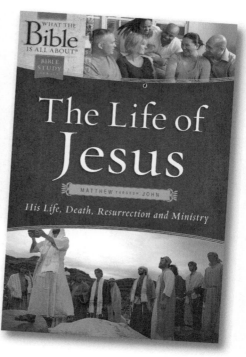